CASE STUDIES IN
CULTURAL ANTHROPOLOGY

GENERAL EDITORS
George and Louise Spindler
STANFORD UNIVERSITY

THE LUGBARA OF UGANDA

Tom

fram John.

Jan. 1965.

THE LUGBARA
OF UGANDA

BY

JOHN MIDDLETON

Northwestern University

HOLT, RINEHART AND WINSTON

NEW YORK   CHICAGO   SAN FRANCISCO   TORONTO   LONDON

Foreword

About the Series

These case studies in cultural anthropology are designed to bring to students in the social sciences insights into the richness and complexity of life as it is lived in different ways and in different places. They are written by men and women who have lived in the societies they write about, and who are professionally trained as observers and interpreters of human behavior. The authors are also teachers, and in writing their books they have kept the students who will read them foremost in their minds. It is our belief that when an understanding of ways of life very different from one's own is gained, abstractions and generalizations about social structure, cultural values, subsistence techniques, and the other universal categories of human social behavior become meaningful.

About the Author

John Middleton is Professor of Anthropology at Northwestern University. He studied anthropology at London and Oxford, and took his doctorate at Oxford in 1953. Since then he has taught anthropology at the universities of London and Cape Town. He has done field research among the Lugbara and Madi of Uganda (1949-1953), the Shirazi of Zanzibar (1958), and the Ibo of Lagos, Nigeria (1964). He has written *The Kikuyu and Kamba of Kenya* (1953), *Lugbara Religion* (1960), and *Land Tenure in Zanzibar* (1961); and has edited *Tribes without Rulers* (with David Tait, 1958) and *Witchcraft and Sorcery in East Africa* (with Edward Winter, 1963); he has also written several papers on the Lugbara.

About the Book

The author gives the reader a clear picture of the setting of Lugbara behavior in the first chapter, and then leads directly to an analysis of how the Lugbara conceive of their society. In this analysis the spatial dimensions of their social relationships, the lay of their land and the distribution of their dwellings, and their social system are linked with the myths that give these sociospatial relationships depth in time and special meaning. In this way, one gains a functional view of Lugbara society, and one sees how every aspect of Lugbara life— fighting, marriage, the settling of disputes, the disposal of the dead and mourning for them, the exercise of leadership and authority—is interdependent with every other aspect.

It is particularly noteworthy that until very recently the Lugbara settled most important disputes by feud or warfare, but that despite a traditional form of social organization that was highly fragmented and lacked obvious political authority above the local group level, and a high density of population, they were able to control competition between local groups for land, grazing, and water. In this respect, and in others, the Lugbara present an interesting contrast to the Bunyoro, described by John Beattie in this series, and the Swazi, described by Hilda Kuper, for these two societies are held together by a strongly centralized state organization.

GEORGE AND LOUISE SPINDLER
General Editors

Stanford, California
December 1964

Preface

This book is about a people of East Africa who have not previously been studied by an anthropologist, although there are a few published papers on them by colonial administrators and missionaries.

I have tried to present a picture of Lugbara society as it was when I visited them. The primary aim of a social anthropologist is to give an account of the way in which a society is organized, and he can do this only by showing the reader how its members see their world, what they think about it, and how they classify their experience. His understanding of their society, unless it is to be superficial, must be based upon what he is told about it by its members. He may use his eyes, but he cannot interpret what he sees without the help of the people themselves. He is thus concerned with their ideas, concepts, and values, and it is only when he knows something of these that he can understand the ways in which they live together.

I studied the Lugbara for a total period of twenty-four months between 1949 and 1952, and returned for three months in 1953. I chose them as a field of study mainly because so little was known about them. I found them kind and patient people who gave me much help and friendship. I hope that my account of them and the culture of which they are so proud may be taken in a small way as payment of the personal debt I owe them.

I was able to live among them through the generosity of the Worshipful Company of Goldsmiths of the City of London and the Colonial Social Science Research Council, London. Later I was able to spend a year writing up my material at Oxford with aid from the Wenner-Gren Foundation for Anthropological Research, New York. I should like to acknowledge the help of these bodies. I also owe much to Dr. John Beattie, who read early drafts of this book and gave me much valued assistance.

J. M.

Evanston, Illinois
December 1964

Contents

Preface   vii

1. The People and Their Country   1
   The Country, 1
   Contact with the Outside World, 2
   The Economy of Lugbaraland, 6
   Farm and Settlement, 9

2. The Form of Lugbara Society   15
   High People and Low People, 15
   Myth, Time, and Space, 18

3. Family, Clan, and Lineage   25
   The Family Cluster and Its Elder, 25
   The Composition of the Family Cluster, 27
   Notions of Descent, 28
   Clan Dispersal, 29
   Host and Accessory Groups, 32
   Remnant Clans, 34
   The Lineage System, 35
   Rainmakers and Holders of Political Authority, 39

4. The Wider Community   43
   Interlineage Relations and Law and Order, 43
   Feud and Warfare, 46
   Chiefs, Headmen, and the Administration of Justice, 52

5. Marriage and Maternal Kinship   54
   Marriage and Exogamy, 54
   Kin by Marriage, 58

6. Spirit and the Ancestors   61
   Offenses and Sins, 61
   Spirit and the Nature of Man, 63
   Death and Burial, 65
   Death Dances, 69
   Contacting the Soul, 71

7. The Cult of the Dead   73
    The Ritual Position of the Elder, 73
    Ghost Invocation and Vengeance, 75
    Oracles, 77
    The Rite of Sacrifice, 78
    Witches and Sorcerers, 81
    Cult, Accusation, and Ambition, 83
    The Prophetic Cult of Yakan, 86

8. Conclusion: The Changing Society   89

References   93

Further Reading   94

Glossary   96

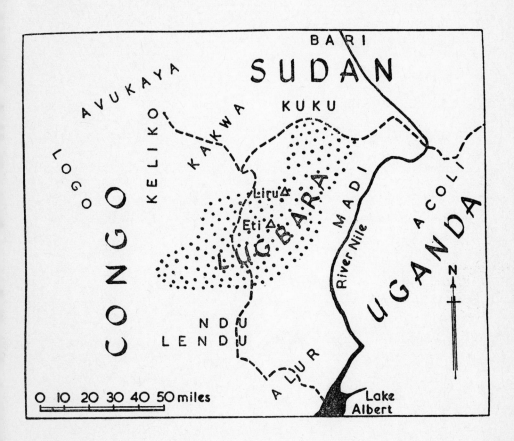

THE LUGBARA OF UGANDA

Lugbara mother making string.

Three co-wives. The eldest wears a traditional iron lip-ring. They are shelling pigeon peas.

A Lugbara market scene. The women in the foreground are selling papyrus mats, rolled up, and those behind sell various pots. The large pots are for beer, the small pots for cooking. The women are mostly wearing the traditional pubic covering of leaves.

A Lugbara homestead, with two living huts and five granaries. Each hut is surrounded by a drainage ditch. Unlike most compounds, this has no hedge around it.

1

The People and Their Country

The Country

T HE LUGBARA LIVE in the present-day West Nile district of Uganda and in the Territoire de Mahagi of the Republic of the Congo (Leopoldville). In 1948, the time of the last census, there were 183,000 Lugbara in Uganda, of whom 160,800 lived in the West Nile district; the remainder consisted of labor migrants working or settled in various parts of southern Uganda (mainly in Bunyoro, Buganda, and Busoga). Congo figures for 1949 give 58,200 Lugbara in that territory and some 2500 Congolese Lugbara working in southern Uganda. There are also about 500 Lugbara in the Yei district of the southern Sudan. The Lugbara thus number in all about 242,000. In this book I shall deal only with the Uganda Lugbara living in their home district of West Nile; the differences between them and the Congolese Lugbara are slight.

The Lugbara are a Sudanic-speaking people. Linguistically their nearest neighbors are the Madi to their east and the Keliko and Logo to their west. Lugbara know of the Madi, Keliko, and Logo as being especially closely related to them, and their languages are mutually intelligible. Lugbara, Madi, and Logo were "like brothers" long ago, while the Keliko are said by Lugbara to be descended from a Logo man who married a daughter of one of the founding ancestors of the Lugbara people. To the north are the Nilo-Hamitic-speaking Kakwa and Kuku, who are also said to be descended from the same founding ancestors, and many of whose clans have the same names as do Lugbara clans. Culturally, if not linguistically, all these peoples are alike. To the south are the Nilotic-speaking Alur, and the Sudanic-speaking Ndu and 'Bale. Lugbara tell myths of the relationships between all these peoples and themselves, although not all are myths of origin. Some, as in the case of the ethnically unrelated Alur, merely give reasons for the two peoples being contiguous and hostile.

These peoples are usually called "tribes," but this does not mean that

1

they are very clearly defined units, nor are they single political entities. They are rather clusters of people who recognize themselves as being culturally distinct from their neighbors. Many of them share the same clan names and may intermarry; people living near the boundaries usually speak their neighbors' languages. Nonetheless, there is never any question as to where the boundaries lie, although, of course, these may change in time, because of population movements and migrations.

The Lugbara live mainly along the line of the Nile-Congo divide, which at this point is also the political boundary between Uganda and the Congo. The divide rises from just under 4000 feet above sea level in the north, where Uganda, Congo, and Sudan meet, to over 6000 feet in the south; most Lugbara live between 4000 and 5000 feet above sea level. They extend eastward to the escarpment which divides the highland region of the watershed from the wooded lowlands of the Nile valley, less than 2500 feet above sea level. The lowlands are occupied by the Madi, although some small Lugbara groups spill over into them. In the north the escarpment ceases and the Lugbara extend to the Sudan border over the low-lying Aringa plains. To the west there is a broken escarpment which forms the boundary between the Lugbara and Keliko, beyond whom are the kingdoms of the Mangbetu and the Azande. To the south lies Alurland, high, broken country at the northern end of Lake Albert.

The Lugbara highlands are clearly marked off from the surrounding areas, and to the traveler in this part of Africa they are very distinctive. Almost all of Lugbaraland except for the bush-covered area of Aringa in the north consists of open and almost treeless rolling plains. Every mile or so there are small permanent streams and rivers, flowing into either the Nile to the east or one of the tributaries of the Uele to the west. Between streams are small hogsbacks, row upon row receding into the distance, many crowned with clumps of recently planted eucalyptus or cassia trees but otherwise almost unwooded. Unlike most tropical African bush country, this area is green and fertile. Across the open country one can see for vast distances, except in the dry season from December to March, when there is too much haze. In the center of the country rise the two great masses of Mounts Eti (Wati on most maps) and Liru. On the southern borders stand Mount Luku and a string of smaller hills which form part of the Madi escarpment. These mountains are visible from every part of Lugbaraland in clear weather and have a conspicuous place in Lugbara mythology. The heart of Lugbaraland is this plateau bounded by the watershed and the circle of mountains Liru, Eti, and Luku. On their plateau the Lugbara have lived isolated from their neighbors and the outside world.

Contact with the Outside World

The Lugbara have been administered sporadically since 1900. At that time this area to the west of the Nile was part of the Lado Enclave, which had been leased in 1894 by the British to the État Independant du Congo. The southern Sudan had been subjected to various degrees of Arab and European influence throughout most of the nineteenth century, but the Lugbara highlands were hardly affected by direct contact with the outside world. By 1885 Egyptian stations had been established among both the Kakwa and the Keliko and at several points along the Nile, but there were none in Lugbara. Emin Pasha stayed at Wadelai on the Nile from 1885 to 1889 and had a Lugbara servant and several Lugbara porters (some of whom were still alive in 1952), but he did not penetrate the distant highlands. The northern Lugbara today speak of four parties of Arabs who entered their country before the Belgians came in 1900, some of whom had contact with the more important Lugbara men. But the Lugbara were never seriously troubled by outsiders except right on the northern and eastern borders of their country, and they escaped the terrible fate at the hands of Egyptian and Sudanese slavers that met most of the small tribes of the southern Sudan.

In 1900 the Belgians began to administer the region, opening several posts, of which one, at Ofude, to the west of Mount Eti, was in Lugbara country. Ofude was occupied for five or six years and the garrison then withdrawn. There were four or five European officers, who rarely left the shelter of the encampment, and a detachment of Congo African troops. Relations were generally hostile and there was much raiding for cattle and grain by the troops. The Ofude Lugbara still tell of the brutality and thieving tricks of the soldiers, aided by some of the Lugbara lineage heads and wealthier men whom the Belgians made *Makoto* ("chiefs"). Their rule was lightened by the excitement of raiding the post and shooting arrows at its occupants by night, but Lugbara speak of this regime as a cruel one that did nothing but bring them troubles.

The Belgian administration introduced agents or "chiefs" with wider powers than any that had existed in the indigenous society. These men were the followers of a prophet, Rembe, a Kakwa living about forty miles north of Lugbara, who had appeared a few years before. He dispensed sacred water in an effort to relieve the tribes of the area from cerebro-spinal meningitis, rinderpest, Arabs, and Europeans; because all four calamities appeared at the same time they were causally interconnected in Lugbara thought. These men had all been important men before Rembe, and when the Belgians asked for the leading men of authority they came forward. As members of a cult meant to control European power they seemed the obvious persons to deal with the Belgians. They were made chiefs and paid for their services in cattle, thus being made rich beyond all Lugbara notions. They are said to have started the present practice of marrying wives with cattle, and had far more wives than had anyone previously. One or two had over fifty wives. Lugbara say that it was these men who first began to "spoil the land" and were responsible for so much of the trouble that has since befallen them. The Europeans and their troops came from outside the social system and were at first not assimilated into it; they behaved badly but then they merely behaved as Europeans and soldiers always did. In fact the Belgians are remembered as kindly men who spent most of their time "drinking gin and tea." The "chiefs," who were the people directly responsible for collecting levies, abused their traditional powers, forgot their traditional responsibilities to the people, and behaved in an upstart and greedy manner. It was toward them that most hostility was directed. It is significant that the word generally used to refer to Europeans, *Mundu* ("rifle"), also refers to chiefs and other Africans employed in the administration. It means essentially a person whose position is ultimately supported by government power. Lugbara date the beginning of the evil days they say have befallen them from this time, and compare the evil present with a perfect past. The year 1900 is a convenient base line by which Lugbara measure the social changes of today.

In 1908, after the death of King Léopold II of the Belgians, the area became part of the Sudan. The effect was slight, although labor service and taxes were introduced over small areas. The Lugbara say that "work and rupees" were their lot in those years. It was at this time that the area became the scene of elephant-poaching on an immense scale, with ivory being taken by traders of all nationalities and without supervision or control; there was doubtless much effect on Lugbara daily life, but it is no longer possible to discover details.

In 1914 the southern portion of the Lado Enclave passed to Uganda, and A. E. Weatherhead took over the administration of the "New Areas," building a station at Arua, the present headquarters. Aru station in western Lugbara, which had never been part of the enclave and so has always been in the Congo proper, was opened about the same time, and the first shopkeepers, Arab and Indian, appeared. Weatherhead is still remembered vividly by the Lugbara, who describe his appearance and behavior in detail. "He was a little man but very fierce, and walked among us without guns," it is said. He waged a continual war against Lugbara groups for the first few years, as his early reports show, to "persuade" them to send representatives to Arua. He refers to the Lugbara as "wild and untractable," and as "shy and unorganized," requiring "severe measures" before submitting to administration.

During the First World War taxation was started, and consumer goods were introduced by traders. In addition, cerebro-spinal meningitis, smallpox, and later Spanish influenza, appeared, together with outbreaks of rinderpest, and the Kakwa prophet Rembe returned. He taught that the drinking of his sacred water would drive out disease and Europeans and bring back their cattle and dead ancestors. He also temporarily introduced a new form of organization to Lugbara. The cult was known as *Yakan,* or the "Allah water cult," and culminated in a rising at Udupi in 1919, after which most of the Belgian-appointed chiefs, who had been reappointed by Weatherhead, were found to have been involved and were arrested and deported. Since then administration has been outwardly peaceful.

Weatherhead appointed "native agents," mostly Sudanese from the remnants of Emin Pasha's troops who had settled in various parts of Uganda. They maintained liaison between the district commissioner, the chiefs, and the local population, and were not withdrawn from the West Nile district until the mid-1920s. Since then local administration has been in the hands of the chiefs. Today in the West Nile district (which includes the Alur, Madi, and Kakwa, as well as the Lugbara) there are five Lugbara county chiefs (*opi* or *sultan*), each with about five subcounty chiefs (*wakil* or *joago*) under him. Under these are parish chiefs *(mukungu)* and village headmen *(nyapara)*. Only these last two are today representative of any indigenous groupings. Chiefs' councils were instituted in 1948 and represent clan and lineage groups as well as factional interests such as local Christians and Muslims. Today all these posts are elective by popular vote, and there is also a superior district administration, in which posts are open to all tribes of the district. In the Congo there is a similar organization. There are five *makoto,* four of whom have very small chiefdoms and one of whom has a large territory and is the most important of all the Lugbara chiefs. Under them are *okils,* and under them *kapita* or headmen.

Today, with the independence of both territories, much more stress has been laid upon elections, and branches of the main political parties have appeared. The Uganda Lugbara were strong supporters of the Uganda Democratic Party, which provided the first self-governing administration of the country and is now in opposition; the Congo Lugbara were supporters of the late Patrice Lumumba.

Missions—the Africa Inland Mission (Protestant) and the Verona Fathers (Catholic)—entered the area in the 1920s, the former from the Congo and the latter from the Sudan. They have many small bush schools and several larger stations with European staffs. It is difficult to assess their influence, and indeed it cannot be considered apart from that of general European contact. Lugbara regard missionaries as *Mundu* and see them as agents of the power of the government which is in many ways antagonistic to the traditional systems of authority. Attendance at schools varies considerably from one area to another, and most children leave school after only two or three years. But the general effect of the missions has without doubt been very great, for they have acted as a channel through which European ideas and objects have been introduced to the people, as well as providing new religious and moral notions. Perhaps most important is their role as the only source of western education, indispensable to anyone who wishes to enter the modern power system of Uganda. Most Christians practice both some form of Christianity and many traditional rites, and find little difficulty in reconciling them. They are significant in different situations, and it can be said that for all but a minority of Lugbara their traditional religious and moral beliefs are still accepted and the rites associated with them still practiced. There has been no governmental prohibition of rites, as in some other parts of Uganda.

There are also several thousand Muslim Lugbara. Arua Town has a population of 3000 so-called Nubis, who are said to be the descendants of Emin Pasha's troops, but the term applies to any recently converted Lugbara man or a Lugbara girl who marries a Nubi. Their role as traders and hawkers has given them an important economic position in the district.

Lugbara still carry on their traditional way of life much as they have always done, and consider the outside world as something quite distinct from their own. Even though since the last war the effects of labor migration and of economic and political development schemes have become marked, for most of the adult population the government, whether European or that of an independent Uganda, is still a novelty, something extraneous and strange, and existing for some purpose of its own. All old men remember the pre-European era from their youth, and have taken part in feuding and warfare. The proportion of Lugbara women who have never seen a European is still very high, and those who have ever heard one speak or seen one closely are only two or three in a hundred. When young Lugbara men go as labor migrants to the south (or when they went to Burma as soldiers in the last war) they behave as members of that society in which they temporarily live. When they return to their homes they relapse into the expected mode of behavior of young Lugbara adults. This may not be the same as it was fifty years ago, but it is still largely traditional. Lugbara are still regarded generally in Uganda as being among the most untouched people of the country; as the older men and women die, the situation will change markedly as the younger, educated people come into their own.

The Economy of Lugbaraland

Lugbaraland is a plateau that is divided into low ridges by the many small streams that thread their way across it. The tops of these ridges are often denuded of soil, exposing the grey granitic outcrops used as drying platforms for grain and cassava. The total soil depth is seldom greater than 4 feet, and although the soils vary considerably within Lugbaraland there are few parts with really poor soil. The rainfall is plentiful, averaging 54 inches a year. It is fairly evenly distributed, and except for the dry season from December to early March there are no periods without rain. August is the month of highest rainfall, although the rains that are important in the agricultural cycle are those that fall in March–April and October–November. Seasonal differences are not considerable enough to lead to transhumance or to have any marked effect on social life, except that in the dry season there is little work to be done in the fields, and beer and food are more plentiful after the main harvest period of July–August than at other times. Formerly there were periodic famines at the end of the dry season, recurring every ten years or so, which can be dated by the marriages of "cheap" wives who fled from famine areas and were married in return for shelter. Almost any genealogy will include one or two of these women. The last famine was in 1942–1943, and since then the compulsory planting of cassava and the setting up of reserves of eleusine at subchiefs' headquarters have reduced the chances of others in the future.

The density of population is high for African subsistence farming. In parts of central Lugbaraland there are 250 people to the square mile; in the less fertile northern and western areas the figure is only 20, and the average for all Lugbaraland is about 150 to the square mile.

The Lugbara are predominantly cultivators, although cattle, goats, sheep, and fowl are kept in most areas. The varieties of crops grown and methods of farming vary with differences in climate and soil types. The traditional crops are eleusine (the staple), sorghum, simsim, various peas and beans, groundnuts, pumpkins, sugar cane, bananas, and many other plants. Since the 1942–1943 famine it has been compulsory for every man to grow a field of cassava, and today this is fast becoming the staple; it is also an easy crop to grow for a woman whose husband is away on labor migration, as it can be stored in the ground and has a high yield. Much maize is grown, mainly for beer making. Lugbara cannot grow cotton except in the eastern part of their country, as other areas are too high for it. A good deal of tobacco is grown for cash.

Meat and milk are unimportant in diet; fowl is eaten, but eggs are given only to infants, because it is thought that adults may become sterile by eating them. Game is no longer found in most of the highlands, but is plentiful in the Madi lowlands and the plains of northern Lugbaraland. Fish are found in streams and caught by nets. Ants are an important article of diet; the sound of women and children beating for ants is heard every evening at the beginning of the rainy season. Many wild herbs and fruit are gathered, the most important of which is shea butter nut.

Formerly men went naked or wore skins, but today most men have some form of European clothing. At the time of my stay almost all women still wore the traditional pubic covering of leaves or grasses, which are cut and made into bunches daily, although there are some types of grass which may be used for a longer period. Most younger women also had a few pieces of cloth and often wore the white skirts found among the Alur. Today most younger women also wear European- or Ganda-style dress for festive occasions.

Iron is smelted by Ndu smiths, and only rarely by Lugbara. The main source of iron was formerly in Ndu country, in the Congo, although there are supplies in Kakwa to the north. It was usually obtained by Ndu themselves or by small parties of Lugbara. It would seem that the amount of iron in the form of artifacts which could be resmithed when required has been almost adequate for local needs. Expeditions were made to obtain the rough lumps of ore called *unzi,* which were used as bridewealth before the use of cattle for this purpose. Today iron hoes are imported and when worn out are used as raw material by the smiths, who set up their homesteads and hearths scattered across Lugbaraland. Clay for pots, wood, ocher, chalk for whitewash, materials for basketmaking, and the few other natural products used in traditional Lugbara economy are all obtainable locally over most of the country. Where they are not, as in the case of papyrus for matting, which is found in only a few remote places, they are obtained by parties of women. Such resources are not claimed by the people living near them. Others can collect them if they desire, although relations of personal friendship play some part. Oracle poisons from the Congo and rainstones from the Sudan are collected by men. Blood brotherhood is unknown, but people travel great distances by invoking indirect ties of kinship. They visit distant kin who send them on in turn to their kin, who may send them on again in their turn. In this way they are given hospitality and protection.

Although there has always been a certain amount of traveling and trading across tribal boundaries, for special commodities, everyday traditional requirements can be satisfied locally within a small neighborhood. It is thus possible for a very small territorial group to exist economically with only very slight recourse to external trading. There is also little specialization. Smiths, women potters, and occasional woodcarvers are the only specialists in material artifacts and can usually obtain raw materials in the neighborhood of their own homes. Other household articles of a traditional kind are made by the women as they want them. Apart from modern consumer goods imported from outside Uganda the objects which have to be obtained from outside the area are few.

There is little ecological difference between the various parts of Lugbaraland as far as traditional crops and materials are concerned, and there were no markets for local exchange before about 1925. Today there are markets at all subcounty chiefs' headquarters, with a large trade in foodstuffs and exchange of small local surpluses. This is centered around the growing of maize for beer brewing, the staple cottage industry. Maize was introduced into the area about 1925. Before then beer was made of millet only, but maize has ousted millet as the popular material. Beer brewing is the only family occupation that cannot be planned in advance and so catered for by seasonal planting, because the drinking of beer is an essential concomitant of all rites and ceremonies, as well as of visiting between kin and friends. Formerly households were larger than they are today, and the needs for beer millet could normally be met from within the household. Today this is far less common, and trade in maize is therefore necessary for every family. Trading is also done in markets in soap, tobacco, kerosene, and other goods, as well as in pots, grinding stones of granite, papyrus mats, and other articles made by energetic and skillful women, although any woman can make these things if she wishes. Most imported articles are also sold at the few African shops at the smaller townships in rural areas and at Indian and Arab stores at the one or two larger centers. The African shopkeepers also set up stalls in markets in their area. Besides dealing in trade goods they also act as distributors of cash and give credit, and are thus more than mere petty shopkeepers. Most of these little shops have a sewing machine for making clothes, and some of them have lorries in which they collect small surpluses of export crops and thereby act as middlemen between the peasant producers and the larger Indian traders in the towns.

Traditionally Lugbara had no currency, exchange being by barter. In recent years Lugbara have become involved in the money economy of the rest of Uganda, with the introduction of taxation, in the Congo part in 1912 and the Uganda part in 1918, and the growth of a demand for consumer goods which can only be acquired for cash. The society is no longer economically self-sufficient. This process has been marked since about 1925, when Lugbara began to go outside their own district to earn money. The rapid expansion of southern Uganda dates from that time, and the West Nile district and adjoining parts of the Congo and Sudan have become peripheral areas supplying labor to the industries and plantations of the wealthy south. In 1951, out of a total

Lugbara population of some 242,000, there were 14,000, or 5.7 percent, in the south. Most of these were men, about 20 percent of the adults being absent at any one time. The absentee rate varies from one area to another, due to several factors, of which the most important is land scarcity, there being a higher absentee rate in the densely occupied parts of central Lugbaraland than in other areas. The type of migration also varies. Some men go to work for wages on contract and return after a year away; others go to settle and to grow their own cash crops in the south, which the Lugbara regard from this point of view as an extension of their lands which may be used to make money. Many of the latter take their wives with them and eventually become "lost" to their kin, but the great majority return with money to pay taxes and buy consumer goods.

Farm and Settlement

The first detailed account of Lugbaraland was written by the Sudan government officer in charge of the area in the years immediately after 1908. He was an acute observer, and wrote of Lugbara (Stigand 1925:19, 89):

> The country to the south (of Kajo Kaji) however, still remained in a disintegrated state; only a few of the chiefs, and those almost entirely at the north end of the country, have any number of followers, or authority. The rest of the tribe is split up under numberless petty chiefs, acknowledging no superior. . . . In 1912 I counted over one hundred so-called chiefs in the comparatively small area between the Koshi and the Alla rivers.

Here he was describing the northern Lugbara. Of central Lugbaraland he wrote:

> To the south of Wati (Mt. Eti) . . . there are an immense number of little communities, some under petty chiefs having only a few dozen followers, and some under no chiefs at all. These are mostly Lugware, but towards Mount Baker (Luku) they gradually merge into Madi. The disorganization of this part of the country was so complete that it was absolutely unparalleled by anything I have seen elsewhere, or heard about. . . . On pitching camp near a village, people would come out and stand in a group about two hundred yards or more distant and watch proceedings. Every time anyone approached them, or shouted to them to come and speak to us, all would turn and fly, coming back later when they found that they were not followed. It was generally only on the second day that they became so bold as to come near enough to speak to, and not till the third day that one was able to buy food from them. As the community was very small, this meant only a few little baskets of flour. On moving to another village only a mile or two away, one would have to go through the whole of this exasperating game again, as there was seldom any communication between neighbouring villages. Each little group was perfectly isolated.

At the time Stigand traveled through the country only a small area below Mount Eti had been subjected to any degree of influence by the Belgian administration, and there had been a few years of ivory-poaching when the area had been virtually unadministered. Stigand thought that it had been disorganized by Arab slavers, but it is certain that they never penetrated this far. There is no reason to doubt that this description was substantially that of the traditional society. This type of fragmentary organization seems in fact to be typical of most of the small societies of the southwest Sudan and northeast Congo, except for the states of Zande and Mangbetu. In Uganda this type of organization is found only among the Lugbara and the Kakwa, although it would appear that the Madi also formerly may have had this kind of system (Middleton 1955).

Lugbara live today in a way very similar to that described by Stigand. This is a country of peasant cultivators, living at a high density of population. It is not bushland roamed by animals, but farmland filled with huts and fields. In the dry season and after the main harvesting, from August onward, the huts stand out in the landscape amid cleared fields. But while the crops are growing the compounds may be almost hidden in the dense crops—the larger varieties of sorghum are usually seven or eight feet high—and the appearance of the country is quite different. At this time there is rain and the atmosphere is clear, so that one can see great distances across the farms and settlements; but in the dry season there is much haze and one may not see more than a mile or two, and the land is no longer green but parched and dry. Homesteads are scattered across the ridges of this open upland country. The Lugbara are polygynous, although over 60 percent of the married men have only one wife, and each wife has her own hut, granaries, and fields. In the compound there are three granaries for a wife, one each for eleusine, sorghum, and legumes, and occasionally a woman has another for grains already mixed for beer brewing, and a small high granary for groundnuts. In a polygynous household the husband may have a hut for his own use, mainly for the entertainment of guests. Today the huts of one husband, with their granaries, typically form a distinct compound, separate from other compounds of related men, and surrounded by its own hedge of euphorbia, climbing beans, pumpkins, and other plants. In the more recently settled areas in southern Lugbaraland, where the compounds of immigrants have become intermingled on the ground, each wife of a polygynous husband usually has her own hut in its own separate compound, away from those of her co-wives.

Physically the compound is the most distinctive unit, a cluster of huts and granaries standing alone, surrounded by its fields. The term used for it is *aku* or *'buru,* referring to the floor of mud and dung kept clean by daily sweeping, and on which the everyday life of the women is conducted. There is usually only one entrance to the compound. Inside the compound are the dwelling huts and granaries, under which are the ghost and other shrines and magical plants. The three upright stones of the fireplace, the center of the women's activities, are placed in a sheltered corner of the compound floor. The word *lico* is often used to refer to large compounds, especially when talking of those of the past, which were larger than those of today. *Lico* means literally "hedge" and is used for the circular hedge set around a compound or a cattle kraal, built near the homesteads and shared by several families of the same lineage.

Aku, 'buru, and *lico* refer to a single residential settlement of any size, from a homestead containing the hut of one wife to that containing the huts of a family group of three or four generations. Besides the living huts there is sometimes an unwalled cooking hut or shelter, and in any group of related compounds there is usually a girls' hut where the unmarried girls sleep with their lovers, and where guests may sleep also.

Lugbara recognize different types of ground: uncultivated land; ground left fallow for a few years; new fallow after cropping which has not yet regained its fertility; later fallow which shows by the presence of certain plants that its fertility has been restored and it is again ready for hoeing; newly cleared and hoed land which is being left for a few months before second hoeing and planting; and so on. All these have specific terms. Lugbara know that different crops need different soils and rotations. Crops are rarely grown in pure stands, and each crop is grown with certain others. Those in a single field are chosen with regard to maintaining soil fertility and ease of harvesting—the crops ripen consecutively in the single field. The crop rotations depend on the nature of the crop varieties and other factors—variance in growing times, recognized fertilizing qualities (e.g., legumes and cassava, which are known to fertilize and clean a field), their ability to provide shed leaves as a mulch, and so on.

Each homestead, occupied by a single wife, has three types of fields: the *amvu akua* (fields at home), the *amvu amve* (fields outside), and the *yimile* (riverine or irrigated fields). The last have high fertility and are used for sweet potatoes, maize, sugar cane, and bananas, and are given very short fallow periods. They are irrigated by small channels cut to take water from a permanent stream running between two ridges. Home fields are fertilized with ashes and manure and are used for the more demanding crops, especially the white sorghums used in beer brewing. Outside fields are not fertilized and are used for the staple, eleusine, grown with sorghums, simsim, and pigeon pea. The rotation cycles are different for each type of field, and only the outside fields can be said ever to be under a system of shifting agriculture; the others are farmed permanently. Outside fields are traditionally cultivated for two or three years and then revert to bush. They are usually opened after three years' fallow, but the length of fallow depends on soil fertility, and some fields may be left for as long as ten years. Home fields have a far higher proportion of cultivation to fallow. Some crops are also grown on the rubbish dumps outside the compounds, and on old hut sites, but these are outside the main agricultural system, as not all homesteads possess them; they are used particularly for tobacco for home consumption (that for sale to tobacco traders is grown on home or outside fields). Fallow is used for grazing, and there are also specific grazing areas, usually where the soil is known to be too thin for permanent cultivation.

Generally men open and clear the ground, which is the heavy work, and women weed and harvest. Both men and women sow, depending on the crop. Men do most of the work on cash crops, particularly tobacco. Men also clear the irrigation channels in the riverine fields. Once harvested the crops belong to the wives, who are responsible for their care and use, although men take the cash crops.

The riverine land is that which is traditionally scarce. In the past there was ample room for other types, but today the outside farms have also disappeared. Nevertheless, the average amount of land needed for each wife has remained constant. Throughout Lugbaraland, despite all differences of crop type and rotation and agricultural methods, the average amount of land cultivated per head in 1953 was the same, between 2400 and 2500 square yards. Fields may be scattered, but rarely lie outside the boundaries of a settlement's traditional field area. This scattering is due to differences in soil type and water supplies. Each wife should have fields of all types and of equal fertility to those of other wives of the group. These requirements mean that there is a fairly fixed relation between the number of wives of the group and the extent of its territory. It means also that there is a maximum size for a single farming group. Once a group's territory has no more of any single type of field within reasonable walking distance, any increase in the number of its wives may lead to the dispersal of its huts. It seems that typically the wives of up to twenty adult men can share a single stretch of land. In the case of some wives' finding it difficult to obtain all three types of land, the opposition between them leads to quarreling and often to accusations of poisoning and other behavior through which the jealousies of the wives of a group are expressed. A man with more than one wife prefers to put the various types of his wives' fields together, to make his work of clearing, burning, and hoeing easier and to avoid quarreling between his wives as to which one has been given the best land and has received the greatest and most careful labor. But men say that the wives still quarrel, such is the nature of women, and prefer to have their plots separated. The husband usually has his way in this respect and this provides one of many rationalizations for the hostility of co-wives. It is as good a rationalization as any, but men grumble over their beer gourds that in the end it all comes back to women's natural propensity to quarrel among themselves and with their husbands.

There are, however, various ways in which shortage of a particular type of farmland may be overcome without splitting up the entire group. The traditional way is for single households to move. A man takes up residence with a kinsman elsewhere, usually his wife's or mother's brother. Land shortage is not the only reason for such a move, but case histories show that it is the most common. Such tenants are usually young men who have just married and have no fields available for their new wives. A tenant may not be deprived of his rights over land, which are heritable, until he or his descendants decide to break the tie.

A young man may also go to southern Uganda to work as a laborer for Nyoro or Ganda landlords, for Indian or Ganda employers, or to grow cotton on his own account. This migration is in many ways a form of tenancy. The main reason is to gain cash, but the degree of migration from an area is affected by the degree of land shortage, the areas with the most shortage supplying the most migrants. A balance has been established between the effective population (that is, the population wholly or mainly dependent upon the land for its livelihood) and the availability of farmland. By migrating outside their own country Lugbara are able to borrow and use the soil fertility and land of southern Uganda, and also lessen the land pressure in their own areas. By migrating temporarily the migrants do not break their ties with family and community, but get over the immediate problem of land scarcity: as they grow more senior in the lineage they can acquire land and then send their juniors in their turn.

Traditionally the huts of a residential group formed a single large compound, or perhaps a cluster of compounds with only a few yards of pathway, rubbish heaps and cattle compounds between them. Huts were clustered together and fields dispersed around the hut cluster. Each group had its home fields immediately adjoining it, the outside fields often being a mile or more away, and as much as ten miles in parts of eastern Lugbaraland where land is poor and uncrowded. The largest local group was (and still is) the subtribe (which I describe in a later chapter), averaging some 4000 people living in an area of up to twenty or so square miles. Compounds and home fields were in the center, on the tops of ridges with riverine fields in the valley bottoms between them; and around them were the outside fields and grazing areas. The subtribal territory was divided among component groups, each separated by its own belt of home fields, and occasionally by a stretch of outside fields as well.

This traditional system has changed almost everywhere in recent years. As soon as land becomes locally scarce three developments can occur. These may be proliferation of tenants (today including the labor migrants) as I have said. Whole groups may move and settle elsewhere in empty land, but this is rare since there is little unused land except on the periphery of the country, and Lugbara do not like to move far, so that in the crowded center this course is not often taken. Or the type of farming may change. In much of central Lugbaraland outside fields have almost vanished, as have grazing grounds except in those parts where the soil is too thin to be used for cultivation. Crops that were grown formerly on outside fields are now grown on home fields, where crop rotations are lengthened to accommodate them. Areas formerly used as outside fields are now used for compounds and new home fields. This has meant that the pattern of settlement has changed also. The former peripheral areas of outside fields are now occupied both by tenants from other groups (about a quarter of the average group's land is today so occupied) and by members of the group itself, who have moved from the center of the territory to other parts of it. The traditional pattern of large hut clusters has changed to one of scattered homesteads, each belonging to the wives of a single man or set of brothers only. With such a pattern it is easier to assure a satisfactory distribution of fields between wives. In addition, this pattern permits a higher density of effective farming population. Another factor is polygyny. Lugbara say that formerly there was more polygyny than today, when 63 percent of married men have only one wife. This is clearly an opinion that cannot be proved, due to lack of reliable evidence for the past, but if correct it provides a further reason for the dispersal of homesteads.

Government regulations also affect the pattern of settlement. Traditionally the distribution of Lugbara settlement was always in a state of slow change. The people say they came from the north or northwest and when the Europeans entered the country they seem still to have been drifting southward. There were no stable boundaries between local communities, and an expanding group could acquire control over an area at the expense of a contracting group. Today the government has fixed boundaries between subtribes at the places where these were when it created chiefs, and has tried to stabilize territorial movement. Today men can still show where their fields, grazing grounds, and former village areas used to be "before the Europeans came." There has also been a considerable increase in population. One consequence has been an ever-increasing disparity between the distribution of population and that of land, so that instead of the density of population varying according to the carrying capacity of the land of any one place, there is now serious maldistribution of population to land. The people of one community may be living at a far higher density than those of neighboring ones. Boundaries are fixed and people who attempt to move across them (as they would traditionally have done) are haled before a government chief as troublemakers. This has affected the traditional process of dispersal of local units according to their land requirements. It has led to an increase in the incidence of individual tenancy, because although a group cannot cross a chiefdom boundary an individual tenant may do so if he has kin on the other side.

2

The Form of Lugbara Society

High People and Low People

IN THIS CHAPTER I show how the Lugbara conceive of themselves and their own society. All people must be able to do this, but of course each people has its own way of doing it, due to varying historical, economic, political, and other circumstances which for a preliterate society may usually only be guessed at. Here I do not try to reconstruct the history of the Lugbara, but limit myself to what they say about themselves.[1]

Lugbara do not know what the limits of their society are in space, except for a small minority of traveled people employed as government chiefs, clerks, police, and so on. But all people know that the people near and around them are Lugbara, and they can see for many miles across the open Lugbara plateau with the two mountain massifs of Eti and Liru standing in the center. These mountains are at the heart of Lugbara: not that they are in the exact center geographically—Liru is on the Kakwa border—but they are the focus of all myth and genealogy. Lugbara are aware that they do not live in isolation, but are members of a society whose land stretches for a great distance. All these people whose lands are visible are members of a single system, conceptually even if not politically so. Among the Logo to the west in the Congo, the Kakwa to the north in the Sudan, and the Acoli to the east of the Nile, people live in small settlements that are surrounded by bush. Paths lead away through the trees and grass to other settlements that are invisible. There is a sense of isolation and discreteness from them. These countries seem to be almost empty of population by comparison to the densely occupied Lugbara highlands. In Lugbara one lives in a homestead from which one can see the surrounding ridges, each covered with huts and cultivation. One can see the members of neighboring families and lineages in their homes and fields. At night one can

---

[1] For those interested, the best accounts of the Lugbara past are those by Father J. P. Crazzolara (1950–1954) and A. N. Tucker (1940).

see the fires smoldering in their compounds and in the grass-burning season the lines of fires blazing in their fields. One is aware of belonging to a small group set in a system, which includes all the other similar groups spread out across the open country stretching away on all sides to the distant territories of people unvisited and hostile, yet actually visible and thus easily conceived as belonging to one system. Some parts of Lugbara along the Congo-Uganda border are now almost uninhabited, with a thick growth of secondary forest. This was often pointed out to me as being unlike what Lugbara country should be, and as a place to be feared. Compounds are set in open fields. It is only the strips of bush along the larger streams that are allowed to remain, the haunts of *adroanzi* ("the children of Spirit"), creatures to be feared and avoided.

At the center of the Lugbara world are the two mountains. They are the focus of Lugbara myths of creation, which are common to all Lugbara groups. Certain neighboring peoples, notably the Kakwa, also feature in these myths, and are thus brought within the same social system. Lugbara and most of their neighbors could be regarded as a single congeries of peoples. Certainly "Lugbara society" is defined culturally, in terms of slight cultural differences of which the most important is the acceptance of the name "Lugbara" (which has no particular meaning).

The Lugbara speak two main dialects: *Uruleti* (high speech) and *Andraleti* (low speech). I refer to them as High Lugbara and Low Lugbara. The differences between them are marked. High Lugbara is close to Keliko and they are mutually intelligible, near the boundary at any rate, although High Lugbara is not so mutually intelligible with Logo, which is said to be so with Keliko. Low Lugbara is very close to Madi. Low Lugbara cannot be understood by the Keliko, nor High Lugbara by the Madi, and it is not easy for High and Low Lugbara speakers to understand each other if they come from groups widely separated.

Although High and Low Lugbara are intelligible respectively with Keliko and Madi, the latter groups are not Lugbara. Lugbara recognize the close relationship, but there is never any doubt as to the boundary of Lugbaraland, of what I call Lugbara society. This boundary is marked physically by a belt between the Lugbara and the neighboring peoples, which is only very thinly populated. But the principal distinction is a cultural one. There are minor differences in culture, mainly in material culture, within Lugbara. Huts, granaries, ornaments on baskets and gourds, tattoo marks, types of baskets, women's knives, and other features vary every few miles. With them go dialectal variations in pronunciation and vocabulary. These and similar differences are found throughout the Logo-Keliko-Lugbara-Madi belt of peoples. The boundaries of Lugbara are marked more by a coincidence of many variations than by any other factor, except that of their accepting the tribal name Lugbara.

Lugbara say that the speakers of High Lugbara are the Urele'ba (High People), and those of Low Lugbara are the Andrale'ba (Low People). High and Low People are distinguished by linguistic differences in this sense: one could draw a line—although it would be an arbitrary one—on a map and say that to the west of it are High Lugbara and to the east Low Lugbara. But if we do this we are distorting the significance of this division for the people themselves. It is by the concepts of High People and Low People that Lugbara comprehend their society and its position in the wider world. These concepts are focused on the two hero-ancestors, Jaki and Dribidu.

The hero-ancestors are associated with the mountains Liru and Eti. Every Lugbara group of any size has its own genealogy going back ultimately to one of these heroes. People say that the hero-ancestor of the High People is Jaki. This is an axiomatic statement: High People are defined by their being descended from Jaki and by speaking High Lugbara dialects, but the former criterion is the more important. Jaki was the son of Yeke, who lived somewhere to the north and was the third or fourth generation from Gborogboro, the first man on earth. Yeke married two wives, Gbele from Koboko in Kakwa, the mother of Jaki, and Ngada, the ancestors of the Kuku and Bari, according to Lugbara. High Lugbara are thus closely related to the Kakwa, and say that once they spoke the same language but it was forgotten after a "Tower of Babel" which reached to the sky fell down, and their ancestors then learned to speak Lugbara. Jaki came to Lugbara country and his doings and wanderings are associated with Mount Liru, on which he died.

Dribidu is the hero-ancestor of the Low People. He also came from the north, and is often said to be Jaki's brother, but whereas Jaki came directly to Mount Liru via what is now Kakwa country, Dribidu came via the Nile valley and wandered through eastern Lugbaraland. He is associated with Mount Eti, a few miles southeast of Liru. He died a few hundred yards below the main peak and what are said to be his grave, his hut-post holes, and his broken cooking pots are still visible there.

Lugbara relate the wanderings and activities of the heroes at length and in immense detail. They had many sons, who were the founders of Lugbara clans. They are thus significant in being the focal points of relationships between local groups, and stories of their death on the mountains and their burial there are told whenever the relationship between clans is under discussion.

High and Low People are in no way divisions with political functions. But a High group has a sentiment of cultural, linguistic, and territorial closeness with those other groups which its members consider to be High People. The same situation is found among Low groups. These divisions are defined relatively. The west is associated with High People and the east with Low People. The principle of definition is that those groups to one's west are usually High People and those to one's east are Low People. In addition, groups north and south, if far enough away to be beyond the range of everyday contact, are likely to be placed in the other division. A High Lugbara will wave his hand along the horizon and say, "Those people over there and those people over there are all Low People; it is we and these people near us here and the people to the west who are High People. But perhaps some others are High People also, who can know all these things?" Although definition is thus partly by social distance, geographical position is also important. If a group lives near the mountain associated with its division all those groups living anywhere near the mountain will be said to be of the same division; but a group that is far from its mountain may well say that the people living near it belong to the other group, because they are outside the range of immediate social relations. Groups that call themselves High People bury their dead with their heads in the direction of Liru, while Low People bury theirs with their heads in the direction of Eti.

Besides giving each group its place in the total society this definition enables Lugbara to place their society as a unit within the cluster of peoples of the region. Lugbara say that Keliko, Kakwa, and Logo are High People and that Madi are Low People. Lugbara are thus in the center of the cluster. I do not know whether Keliko or Kakwa themselves say that they are descended from Jaki, as Lugbara say they are, but some Madi groups do say that they spring from Dribidu. The peoples to the south, Alur, 'Bale, and Ndu, do not feature in this schematization. Contact with them is recent and even now not intimate, and they are very different in culture. Lugbara society is oriented northwest, toward the peoples with whom they have a common ethnic origin.

We see here the operation of a common principle. All groups of a society can be related genealogically, by Lugbara ways of thinking. The more distant socially, the further back genealogically is the tie that relates them; the closer socially, the closer the genealogical link. Any Lugbara group knows only its own genealogies and something of those of its immediate neighbors, who are always considered to be of the same division. Beyond one's own community little or nothing is known of the genealogies of other groups. Thus the division into High and Low People is a relative one, the distribution of which differs for every group in Lugbara. The historical past of another group's ancestry is irrelevant; what is relevant is its present territorial and social relationship to one's own. It is clear also that in this context social distance is equated more or less with spatial distance. The division into High and Low People is seen in territorial terms.

Myth, Time, and Space

Lugbara say they are descended from the first creatures put on earth by Spirit at the beginning of the world. Lugbara are all "of one blood" *(ari alo),* created by Spirit the creator of men *(Adroa 'ba o'bapiri).* Spirit created a man, Gborogboro, and a woman, Meme, and domestic livestock. Meme had wild animals in her womb. The gazelle broke out and was followed by the other beasts. The name Gborogboro means "the person coming from the sky" and Meme means "the person with a heavy body." After the animals had left Meme's womb Spirit put children in it, according to some versions; others say that she became pregnant after goat's blood has been poured over her legs;[2] and still others say that the pair were taught how to have sexual intercourse,

---

[2] It is said that she did not menstruate. Lugbara believe that conception occurs only in the three or four days following menstruation, so that the pouring of blood "showed" her how to menstruate and like menstruation was followed by conception.

which was followed by conception. Meme bore a boy and a girl. Myths tell that these siblings produced another male and female pair, who did the same in their turn. There were several generations of siblings, after which the heroes, Jaki and Dribidu, were born.

Other myths tell of the separation of mankind from Spirit in the sky, the separation of "black" and "red" (European and Arab) peoples, the building of a Tower of Babel and its destruction, and the appearance of Lugbara and Kakwa and the diverse tribes and languages of men. All these events took place somewhere to the north of Lugbaraland. They are not related to each other nor put into any time sequence except insofar as the creation itself preceded all human activities.

This corpus of myth culminates in the two hero-ancestors coming to the present country of the Lugbara and there begetting sons who were the founders of the present clans. The heroes were not human as men are now. Dribidu means "the hairy one," since his body was covered with long hair. He is also known as 'Banyale ("eater of men"), since he ate his children until he was driven out of his earlier home. He came to the Lugbara highlands and there found a leper woman who gave him fire with which to cook his buffalo meat. He cured her with medicines, the secrets of which are now lost. He then made her his first wife (mothers of his previous children are irrelevant and so not known). He impregnated her, which resulted in feud with her kin and the subsequent payment of seduction fine and bridewealth. He did the same with other leper women, and after begetting many sons died on Mount Eti. Similar myths are told of Jaki.

The heroes were not normal human beings, living in a society and recognizing its values. They mark the appearance of Lugbara society in the form which it has today. The heroes married many women and their sons married wives and had children, thereby becoming the founders of clans. The present-day groups are thus descended from the founders of the original clans, with continual proliferation and amalgamation. The ancestors who feature in these genealogies are always regarded as having been normal social beings who behaved in a way that men do behave and believe they should behave—for the reason, of course, that the ancestors laid it down that they should. All special rights and mystical powers possessed today by certain men of certain lineages— for example, the power to control the rain or to possess certain magical objects —are validated by their having originated at the time of the heroes or of their sons. For Lugbara, their society today is essentially the same as it was at that time.

The several accounts of the creation of the pairs of siblings, the hero-ancestors, and their descendants differ in character. I have given them, very briefly, as though they are parts of a single history. I have never heard Lugbara doing so. Indeed, the differences in their nature make it unlikely that they would be told on the same occasion. The accounts of the creation and of the activities of the siblings before the heroes may be called mythical; those of the heroes themselves present both mythical and genealogical features, that is, they may be placed in either category on different occasions. If we put them on a time scale, the heroes are either at the end of the mythical period or at the beginning of the genealogical period. But to do this is to distort the significance of these accounts. The difficulty is that our own myths and histories are placed on a time scale and therefore all the concepts we use in this context contain a reference to nonrecurrent measured time.

The main difference between the period before the heroes and that after them (the heroes appearing in both periods) is that in the latter the personages are ordinary beings and clan members behaving in the way that people do now, but in the former they behaved in a reverse manner and lived in social isolation in a world in which there were no clans. They committed incest, not yet recognizing ties of kinship; they did not transfer bridewealth for their mates, and ties of affinity and the family as such were not yet recognized; they could do marvelous feats which men can no longer achieve—the first pair of siblings were called Arube ("worker of miracles") and O'du ("miraculous omen"), and the other siblings have names associated with magic or the introduction of techniques by magical means; they are sometimes said to have been born with teeth. Their characteristics are nonhuman or contrahuman. It is with the appearance of the heroes and their begetting sons that human beings became social beings living in a society. Before that they were not members of a society—there was no society, in fact—and they and their world existed in the north outside present Lugbara territory, a territory of which every part is associated in tradition with a particular clan. Before he entered Lugbaraland Dribidu was a cannibal, eating his own children. Once arrived in Lugbaraland the heroes became more or less social beings, but always retained some superhuman and magical qualities. They learned the art of fire making from the leper women, whom they then turned from incomplete women (lepers) into complete and social women by curing and marrying them. I refer to the attributes of the preheroic figures as "inverted." Their inverted and superhuman attributes are indexes of their asocial existence before the formation of an ordered society.

A similar use of myth can be seen in the accounts of the appearance of Europeans in Lugbaraland. The ancestor of the "red" people was Angbau, the brother of Yeke the father of Jaki, so that the red people have a parallel existence to the black people. But this it outside Lugbara society. Those Europeans who enter it are placed in a different category. Those who first came to Lugbaraland are called by various names, but they are all given similar attributes. They were cannibals (as all Europeans are thought to be today except those well known as individuals to Lugbara), they could disappear underground, and they walked on their heads and could cover vast distances in a day by this means. As soon as they were noticed they began to walk on their legs, but if attacked they would vanish into the ground and come up some distance away. They would then move away on their heads. They were thus literally "inverted." I have heard it said that this is still the way in which Europeans behave in their own country "beyond Lake Albert." In 1900 the Belgians came. Myth says that when they came everyone ran away. The Belgians and their cruel and reputedly cannibalistic troops chased the fugitives and found one or two important men hiding in the bushland outside their homesteads; these men were made "chiefs" by the Belgians. Chiefs are often known as the "clients" (atibo) of the Europeans. Since the presence of clients in a homestead is always explained by saying that an ancestor found them "hiding in the grass" outside the homesteads and took them in as "his people," the appointment of chiefs is also explained in these terms. It is hardly necessary to add that in fact they did not run away nor were they found hiding, according to detailed accounts given to me by persons who were there in 1900.[3] Other accounts say that because the Europeans came from outside society, as clients come in time of famine, they were taken in and welcomed by important men who acted toward them as "fathers": they were then made chiefs by the Europeans. It is clear that either version explains the way in which the Belgians and the new chiefs became part of Lugbara society. It is said that the first British administrator, A. E. Weatherhead, could walk across the country at fantastic speeds; no sooner was it thought that he was safely away a hundred miles to the north, and people began to attack his headquarters at Arua or to fight their neighbors, then he would suddenly appear in person among them. He is said to have had powers of personality, courage, and sympathy that could be due only to magic and heroic qualities. "His words were strong" and he impressed them as no other Europeans, before or after him, have ever done.

Since those days Europeans entering the country have had a place in Lugbara society and an expected role to play there. There are different categories of Europeans but they all have fixed statuses. Lugbara can list most of their district commissioners and missionaries since the days of Weatherhead. Other government officers are rarely remembered but it is thought that there is some kind of genealogical or quasi-genealogical tie between district commissioners and between missionaries. I have often heard it surmised that certain Europeans were the sons or sisters' sons of earlier figures. But all these Europeans have behaved in a normal way and have had none of the superhuman qualities of Weatherhead.

For Lugbara time is periodic, reckoned mainly by generations of men, the seasons, the stars, the moon, and the sun.[4] All these phenomena occur at regular intervals and are not placed on a scale of nonreccurrent time. Events that do not recur are not put on a measured time scale. Lugbara myth and genealogy are little related to historical time as we comprehend it. Genealogy explains and validates the social relations between people of the present day. No Lugbara knows much of the genealogies of clans other than his own, since they are for the most part outside his everyday experience. Genealogies deal with social beings as members of a given community, and the ancestors are only significant, and therefore remembered, insofar as the relationships between

---

[3] Accounts of the head-walking Europeans were given to me by men who were eyewitnesses to their arrival. But the necessary use of the idiom of inversion to describe the concept of "asocial" is more meaningful to Lugbara than a dry photographic account.

[4] Unlike many East African peoples, the Lugbara have no age-classes that could provide a measure of passing time.

them validate the present composition of the community. But the ancestors are placed in society, and society itself is given meaning and validity, by myth. Myths in Lugbara deal with personages originally not members of society, beings whose relations with one another are asocial, in that they do not recognize the obligations of kinship and neighborhood. Most of the values and sanctions concerned with social behavior are associated with the cult of ancestral ghosts, and there is no ritual attached to the mythical figures. The myth themes end by certain personages forming or entering the society and receiving a status within it. As the extent of the society increases and new persons are introduced into it, as were the Europeans and their chiefs, they are given identity and status by means of myth. Mythical figures are outside society and genealogical figures are within it, and there are some personages—the heroes and the first district commissioner—who belong to both myth and genealogical tradition. The two are thus linked and derive significance and validity from each other. But to set them into a scale of historical time is misleading, because the events are related to each other not by their temporal relationships but by the social relationships between the personages whose activities compose the myth and genealogical tradition.

We put the events I have described in a scale of time. Similar concepts are used by the Lugbara to refer to a scale in space. The same thematic pattern, with normal members of society at the center, then a belt of quasi-members who possess some superhuman and inverted attributes, and beyond them the remainder of the world peopled by inverted beings, may be discerned in Lugbara notions of the world as it is today. The relations between people and groups within a local community are expressed and validated by genealogical tradition. Beyond the community live other people. One can see the trees on their ridges and the flames and smoke of their field-burning; one can often hear the distant drumming from their dances. They may be Lugbara or other peoples, but in the context of social distance this is not relevant. Social ties cross tribal boundaries. What is relevant is that they are beyond the limit of everyday social relations. They are given certain attributes, of which the most common is the possession of magical powers and medicines. Although the limit of everyday relations cannot always be measured, it is usually about ten or fifteen miles away across the open plateau, and the magical beings stretch away to the horizon. If a man has actually visited that far, then the particular people he visits are regarded as exceptions that prove the rule. The anthropologist may see the contradiction in a situation in which groups within distant view of each other may describe each other as being magicians and sorcerers, people with evil medicines and the power to turn into stones and trees on the path when one meets them; but for Lugbara the occasion to see the contradiction does not often arise.

Every household thus sees itself as surrounded first by people like themselves, then by a circle of people whose territories are filled with sorcery and magic and who are evilly disposed toward them, even though it is assumed they are Lugbara. But this is relative: when compared to groups beyond them, who are even worse, the closer strangers appear almost like one's own kin. They are people beyond the bounds of society altogether, and people say of them, "How do we know where they come from, of what deeds they do? We fear them and we do not know them." The most distant of these creatures, beyond the magicians and the sorcerers, are thought to be hardly human in appearance. Although they are never visited, it is known that they walk on their heads. Such are the Logo, the Mundu, the 'Bale, and people beyond them, the areas from which the Belgian troops came. These people eat meat that is rotten, and "bad" meat such as snakes, frogs, hyenas, and other night animals. Peoples such as the Makaraka, the Momvu, the Mangbetu, and the people whom Lugbara know as Niam-niam, the Azande, are all reputed to be cannibals. They walk upside-down, beget children by their sisters, have terrible types of sorcery, and live in the thick forests in ways which Lugbara cannot understand.

These are not mere fairy stories told for amusement, although they arouse both mirth and horror. Lugbara apply one set of concepts, which we can express only in the separate categories of time and space, both to the mythical and genealogical past and to the contemporary social environment. In mythical and genealogical distance any actual or comparative time scale is irrelevant. All myths have the same thematic pattern. Similarly any actual or comparative scale of territorial distance is irrelevant to the spatial categories. The same thematic pattern is found whatever the actual physical distance may be. In both schemes the essential distinction is between the near people, members of one's own

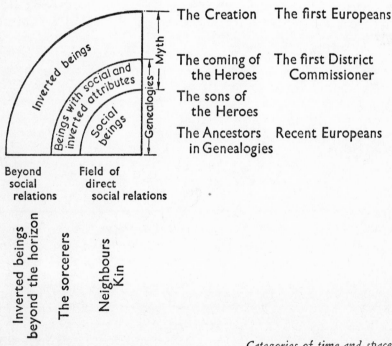

Categories of time and space.

community and neighborhood, and the distant inverted people, who are beyond social relations and outside genealogical tradition. Each community has its own genealogy, known only to itself, but the same corpus of myth is held by all Lugbara. The limits of social relations that are important for any group are defined by mythical inversion.

There are, of course, degrees of inversion, corresponding to degrees of social distance. In general, inverted beings are asocial and their behavior amoral, but degrees of associability and amorality vary. The incestuous cannibals are more inverted than the sorcerers, and are socially more remote, being in fact beyond contact altogether. The more remote the being, the more its behavior is conceived as being the utter negation of that to do with kinship: for an ordinary man to ensorcell someone is at least comprehensible, whereas to eat his own children is not.

3

Family, Clan, and Lineage

The Family Cluster and Its Elder

THE SMALLEST DOMESTIC UNIT is the "hut" *(jo)* occupied by a single wife and her small children. The "compound" *(aku)* is the home of a married man, whether he has one or several wives. Elementary and compound families are grouped into larger residential units which I call family clusters. Each of these has a head, known as *'ba wara* or *'ba ambo* (literally, "big man"), which I translate as "elder."

The family cluster is a small group, generally of about twenty-five people (about six adult men and their wives and children). It is not always a compact unit, though it may be (and probably was in the past). Today it usually consists of a scattered group of homesteads, which may be up to half a mile across. The cluster has its own stretch of land, in which are its compounds, fields and grazing, and its own livestock; and its members have a strong sense of "belonging." When the cluster becomes too large to act as a single family group it may split in two. Thus at any particular time the unit under the authority of an elder may be a single compound family or a cluster of several families. But whatever its size, it has a single elder, and plays the same part within a wider system of similar groups. It is the basic unit of Lugbara society. When a man speaks of "home" *(akua,* literally "at the compound") he refers to the family cluster. When a wife visits her parents and natal kin, she visits all the members of the family cluster into which she was born. Its compounds are "the homes of the ancestors," who are thought to dwell in the earth beneath them.

Lugbara think of the family cluster as being based upon a small lineage. A lineage consists of people descended in one line from a single founding ancestor. Descent may be through men only (patrilineal) or through women only (matrilineal). The Lugbara lineage is patrilineal. A family cluster typically consists of adult men who are members of a single lineage, with their wives (who by the rule of exogamy belong to other lineages), and unmarried chil-

25

dren. It is in this sense that I speak of the lineage forming the "core" of a family cluster. There are both small and large lineages, as we shall see later in this chapter. The family cluster is formed around the smallest, which I call a minimal lineage. The lineage is conceived as permanent, persisting over many generations; the family cluster is not. Land and livestock are vested in the lineage, but rights in them are enjoyed by its living members.

The family cluster is controlled and represented by its head, the elder. Like most Lugbara institutions, the office of elder cannot be very clearly or precisely defined. His status and authority shade into those of the heads of junior families, and these may also be called elders if they are old. But Lugbara always know whether a man is a "real" elder or not, and the term is properly applied only to those men who by virtue of genealogical position in the lineage have the custodianship of certain shrines. All heads of domestic families whose fathers are dead have shrines to the ghosts of the recent ancestors and various spirits. But an elder, besides having the ordinary ghost shrines of his own homestead, also has special shrines for the ghosts of the founding ancestors of the major lineage and the clan (I define these groups below). I call these external lineage shrines. They are built outside the homesteads in a patch of bush, well away from the ghost shrines in the compounds. The elder's spiritual power is associated especially with those shrines that are outside the homesteads and in the bush. This is not a friendly place but is fearsome and even evil. Most men keep away from these external shrines, and only elders venture there.

An elder has certain traditional insignia of office, although today many no longer possess them. The most important is the *ogua,* a special round stool made from a single piece of wood. No one but elders may sit on these stools, and they are inherited. There are other marks of office found in different parts of the country, certain sticks or wands being the most common.

Lugbara define an elder by saying "a man is called the elder because he eats the chest of meat," or "because he eats the tongue," "because he sits on the *ogua* stool," "because he stays with the shrines" (this is partly a reference to his role in war when he stayed behind making offerings to the ghosts during the fighting), "because he cuts meat at the shrines," "because he puts his hand into the shrines." In parts of northern Lugbara he is called *ori'ba,* which in that area means "ghost shrine man." The elder makes the actual offerings at most sacrifices and says the ritual address, and he directs the division of the sacrificial meat. At the distribution certain parts fall to him, to be eaten by him and his chief wife alone. These parts are the spare meat of the chest, the liver, kidneys, testicles, penis, intestines, and usually the tongue. I was told by an elder that "our work is the work of the home," that is, to do with the ghost shrines and the maintenance of peace and good order in the family.

The elder is the senior living descendant of the minimal lineage's ancestors; he is nearest to the most recent of them and is expected to be the first to die and join them. He is a representative of the living members of his lineage to the dead, a role expressed in his powers of cutting and distributing meat. He is also the representative of the dead to their living kin. Thus it can be said that he has two roles which overlap to some degree. He is the ritual representative of the lineage and he is also the head of the family cluster. In the latter role he has religious sanctions over a range of dependants who include people that are not members of his own lineage.

The elder should be the eldest son of the senior, or first, wife of his predecessor. If a married man inherits a widow from his father, then that wife, if she was married first, becomes his senior wife and takes precedence over the wife whom he has already. "You fear that wife of your father because she is like your mother." She would not, of course, be a man's own mother, but one of his mother's co-wives. In such a case, the heir is the first-born son of that senior wife, even if that son is younger than a son of the junior wife, who was in fact the first married to this particular husband. This principle permits succession by both son and brother, and leads to much wrangling and uncertainty as to succession and inheritance.

This rule of succession refers essentially to the mystical power of being able to sacrifice at the shrines as the nearest direct descendant of the dead ancestors. But in fact the elder so appointed may not be regarded as the elder in all situations. If he is young, weak, or poor, he may be replaced in some situations by a close kinsman who is senior, strong-willed or wealthy, who will act as a kind of regent in everyday matters.

The Composition of the Family Cluster

The members of a family cluster consist of three kinds of people. First there are the members of the minimal lineage which provides both its name and its elder. This lineage is usually of three to five generations in depth, with up to three generations of living members, who are the descendants of the lineage founder who is thought to have lived a generation or two earlier than the oldest living man. The lineage includes both men and women, and daughters married elsewhere remain members of it during their lifetime and after their deaths; however, as in most patrilineal systems, the memory of their names fades after a few generations. In all family clusters some men born into them move away to settle elsewhere, temporarily or permanently, but they remain lineage members, as do their patrilineal descendants. They, too, may be forgotten in later years if they live far away, and if ties are not maintained by visiting.

A man is expected to respect his senior kin, both living and dead, a child its parents, a wife her husband, a sister her brother, and a younger sibling an older one. Lugbara define "respect" (ru) as obedience, fear, and affection. It is ambivalent, as they realize very well. A man should love his father, who has brought him up, protected him, and taught him to become a responsible adult, but at the same time Lugbara observe cynically that a man may "hate his father in his heart," because as long as his father is alive he is merely a "youth" and economically dependent. "A man loves his father but he waits for him to die." A father should discipline his sons, yet he does not wish to harm them.

He beats his children when they are small, but once they are adolescent he uses religious sanctions against them for all but trivial offenses. It is said that a man is unwilling to strike his sons with his hand and so he asks the ghosts to do it for him. He acts in many situations as the representative of the dead members of the lineage, who look after the well-being and happiness of their living kin. To the living "our ancestors" are near and vivid, for they are the sources of morality and the focus of lineage identity vis-à-vis other lineages.

The relationship between brothers should be—and usually is—one of affection and mutual help between equals. The same term is used for both elder and younger brothers. To call a friend a "brother" is a compliment, and Lugbara often say that important men who are equal in status, such as rainmakers and chiefs, are "like brothers"—in this phrase there is also the connotation that the "brothers" stand together, possibly selfishly, against outsiders. But Lugbara maintain that most brothers are sometimes jealous of one another over family property, and senior men may compete with their brothers for the ritual status of eldership of the family cluster. In such a case the competition may be fought out quite unscrupulously. A man is expected to protect his sister and give her good advice, and sisters to help their brothers when asked. They help one another particularly in their love affairs, and keep these secret from their parents.

The family cluster also includes the wives of lineage members. The head of a family has domestic authority over his wives and children. A wife does not change her lineage at marriage but remains a member of it and under the care of its ancestors all her life. Sacrifices on her behalf are generally made by her father or brothers to their ghosts, but it is thought that she can also be made sick by the ghosts of her husband's lineage, and in that case her husband's people sacrifice for her. She remains predominantly under her own ancestors' care, and when those of her husband affect her they do so because she is a mother of their descendants rather than because she is a wife. Her position is thus ambivalent: although she never relinquishes her affiliation to her natal lineage and its ghosts, in everyday affairs she is under the authority of the senior men of her husband's group, and her natal family and her own ancestors do not intrude so long as she is well treated and content.

Lastly, a family cluster may include one or two men of different lineages. They are usually the sons or husbands of women who were born into the lineage. For various reasons they prefer to live with their mothers' or wives' kin. They accept the authority of their host elder, but their position, like that of wives, is ambivalent, as they still have close ties with their own natal lineage. There may also be clients, unrelated men who attach themselves to rich men as followers and who may be given their daughters as wives.

Notions of Descent

Lugbara see their society as being descended from the heroes and their sons through long patrilineal descent lines. These lines consist of ancestors who are points of articulation between lineages. They vary in depth from eight to thirteen generations.

All Lugbara descent lines go back to a common set of brother-ancestors, the sons of the heroes. Lugbara think of their tribal unity as being due to ties of "blood" (*ari*). They say they are "one people" and "all one blood", and so different from Kakwa, Alur, Europeans, and others. This blood comes from the Creator Spirit. They use the same expression when speaking of the unity of members of a clan, the group consisting of the patrilineal descendants of a son of one of the heroes. It is generally not used in reference to lineages; of these it is said "people have different bodies, one blood".

Descent is seen as running through both men and women. Patrilineal descent in the direct line can be reckoned for everyone back to the first men placed on earth by Spirit, through one of the heroes and down a direct line of ancestors to living men and women. Descent through women is reckoned for only a few generations, until kin so related are "far away" and forgotten. As far as personal kinship ties are concerned Lugbara see little difference in descent through a man or a woman. If a man is killed his mother runs back to her own people, who come to join in the fighting to avenge his death,

> because his blood came from here, from his mother's brother's people. Now her son has died and left only little children. Truly he is our man. If our daughter had been born a man she would have begotten children here with us, but she bore that child there with her husband. Truly he is our child.

Associated with these notions of descent are those of unisexual characteristics. Lugbara say that a man takes after his father and a woman after her mother. This is axiomatic, despite what are to the observer clear exceptions. Physically it is often true. This notion is not often socially significant with regard to men—witchcraft powers, for example, are not in theory inherited, although a witch's son who behaves like his father in other ways might be thought to be one—but in the case of women is connected with their possession by Spirit. This possession gives an adolescent girl the power of divination, which is inherited by daughters. The society is predominantly patrilineal in bias. Descent through a woman may be significant in lineage affiliation for men, but is not so for women: one female link may be accepted as though it were a male link, but more than one are too weak to be significant in lineage matters. There remains the mother-daughter line which is important neither in inheritance of status or property nor in ritual. It is significant only in the context of divination, which although a socially useful activity is nonetheless associated with evil and is feared.

Clan Dispersal

Lugbara see their society as being made up of clans that have spread out and dispersed from the original clan homes where their founders were begotten by the heroes. Once I was talking about this with an old man, and we had gone to watch ants moving across a path. It was the beginning of the rains and streams of ants were everywhere. He said:

You have heard the words I have said to you. We people are like these ants. Once our ancestors lived separately. Then they wandered among themselves, they wandered across the land like these ants, and now we live together in our little groups. We have come far from the home of our ancestors.

We need not accept clan traditions as relating historically true events, but they are not necessarily untrue in every detail. Most genealogies that tell of past relationships with other groups elsewhere probably reflect actual historical events, although there is no way of telling how far back in time they took place. At least we may accept the general theory of dispersal of groups as told by Lugbara as being true. Besides telling of historical events, genealogies are also used to validate a present distribution of groups which is in a constant state of change and realignment.

There are today at least sixty clans. Their founders were the sons of the heroes. These sons had sons in turn, and their patrilineal descendants form the clans which Lugbara regard as the basic units of their society. They are basic because they are regarded as permanent and above change, although this is not in fact always true. No clan is senior to any other. The order of birth of their founders is unknown, and although they vary in size it is never said that a clan is more important than another merely because it is larger. Each clan has a clan-name, which, like all Lugbara names, has an original meaning that can usually be explained.[1] I use the term "clan-name" to refer also to names given to lineages—many lineages have the same names as do clans.

The members of a clan are dispersed and found in many parts of the country. Since the founding of Lugbara society the descendants of the clan founders, who were the sons of the hero-ancestors, have moved about the country, groups of kin segmenting and moving apart just as they do now. But there is almost always a main part of a clan that has not split up and that still inhabits a territory associated with the clan. It forms what might be called the localized core of that clan, and I call it a subclan. The founder of a subclan is thus the same man as the founder of the clan. A clan is a shadowy group that consists of a subclan living in the clan territory and a number of offshoots that have moved away at various times in the past and now live in other clan territories elsewhere. The subclan is the important unit in everyday matters. In the territory associated with it, and which is given its name, live members of other clans whose ancestors settled there or who have settled there recently themselves. The total group thus formed I call a subtribe, which is also given the name of the subclan. I describe the subtribe later in this chapter. Subclans are segmented into smaller descent groups, which I call lineages. The number of generations given in any genealogy from living people to the clan founders is usually from eight to thirteen. It would be possible to trace the supposed genealogical relationships of any two members of a clan or subclan (and therefore of any two Lugbara

---

[1] Examples are Lariba, "the fig-tree people"; Anyavu, "the eaters"; Anyatibion-ziku, "we do not eat bad vegetables." Most refer to some characteristic of an ancestor in myth or genealogy, although some are place-names only.

anywhere), but this is never done. Kinship ties between individuals are traced only within lineages.

Proliferation of clans and lineages takes place in two ways, as it can be observed if not by the anthropologist at least by Lugbara themselves in the course of a lifetime. These are by the expansion and segmentation of a lineage, and by dispersal of individuals who leave their parental homes and settle elsewhere, founding lineages of their own. These individuals may be accompanied by their domestic families. Proliferation is usually caused by an increase in numbers and is associated with a migratory drift across the countryside in search of more land. The northern and central parts of Lugbaraland have been longer settled than the south, and most movement is, or was, from the densely occupied north to the emptier south.

Lugbara are farmers and people move into areas where there is spare land. With the rotation of crops, families are always moving their farms from exhausted to fresh land, so that they move huts and fields every few years into that part of their neighborhood where there is either more fresh land or least opposition. Where the land is uniformly occupied a group moves into the territory of their most distantly related neighbors. All groups will resent intrusion. One cannot clear land and move into the land of one's close agnates since the elders and (it is believed) the ancestors will object. But to move into the area of an unrelated or less closely related neighbor is less opposed by kinship sanctions and one's immediate kin will give support in any consequent fighting. In addition, men often move away and settle with their mothers' or wives' kin as soon as they are married and need land of their own.

In recent years it has become increasingly difficult for groups to move into their neighbors' lands, since the government now tries to prohibit movement of this sort, which leads to disputes and fighting. The result has been that more men hive off from their home settlements, taking up land either with a maternal or affinal kinsman or in the peripheral areas of the country. As I have said above, many of these are in fact today outside Lugbaraland altogether, in the richer lands of Bunyoro and Buganda.

The general process of migration-drift takes place both by lineage movement, amoebalike, in one general direction, and by the settlement of individuals and their families elsewhere, usually in the less-populated areas to the south. The routes taken during the slow migration of a group across the countryside are told in legend, in which ancestors are said to have lived in certain places—like the heroic myths, migrations distant in time are expressed in narratives of individual travels—and can be seen in the distribution of burial trees. Every important man and woman has a barkcloth tree planted at the head of his or her grave. The grave itself is covered by stones which are left undisturbed for several years. The tree is never cut, nor its wood or leaves used, and the land immediately surrounding it is not cultivated. It is given the personal name of the individual whose grave it marks. These great trees, often several generations old, are a marked feature of the Lugbara landscape, usually standing alone, although in some areas they form part of raingroves and so are not noticeable.

The burial tree of Dribidu is still visible on the mountain on which he is buried. The burial trees of a group's more distant ancestors are usually well outside its present territory, especially in southern Lugbara. In the north they are often still inside the territory, because there has been less recent migration movement there. The migration routes of lineages can be traced across country by the trees of their ancestors. In some cases, of course, as in that of Dribidu, a burial tree is named so as to be consistent with and thereby confirm belief in a myth or legend.

This process of migration-drift has resulted in the dispersal of clans over the countryside. Tradition may not be historically correct in every detail, since details have to fit in with the axiomatic origin of clans near Mounts Eti and Liru; otherwise the process described in tradition may be observed occurring today as it has presumably occurred in the past.

Host and Accessory Groups

I have mentioned that local land shortage may lead people to leave their parental homes and attach themselves to uterine kin, at whose homes they are given land and take up residence. This leads in time to the formation of what I call accessory groups attached to host groups. I prefer the term "host" to terms such as "dominant" or "authentic." In Lugbara they are dominant neither politically nor ritually, except that they give their name to the territory in which they live. "Authentic" implies that accessory groups are not authentic but may claim to be so, which is not true in this case. I have never heard the origin of an accessory group deliberately concealed, but it is possible that in the past this was so, especially when such a group's founding ancestor was in a servile position to the host group, as was a client, usually a poor man without land who attached himself to a wealthy but unrelated man. Inferior origin is sometimes used as a taunt in personal quarrels, but then so is size of a clan that has so dwindled in numbers that it can no longer maintain its own rights, and such groups may be among the oldest and most "authentic" of all. Taunts of this kind reflect numerical weakness rather than inferior origin.

The term for a host group is *kari'ba*, meaning the direct patrilineal descendants of the subclan founder. The terms for accessory groups are variants of words for "stranger"; among High Lugbara I have heard them referred to as "our Madi," that is, as Low Lugbara or strangers.

Accessory groups are usually the descendants of a man who attached himself to a member of the host group, as a uterine or affinal kinsman or as a client. The original host-client relationship was between individuals and is inherited by their descendants. If the tie was one of mother's brother-sister's son then the accessory group remains as "sisters' sons"; if it was one of brothers-in-law, then it remains so, notwithstanding the fact that this tie becomes one of mother's brother-sister's son after one generation; and if it was a tie of clientship then it remains so for several generations, although later this may change to a tie of "brothers."

Groups as well as individuals may move and become attached as accessory groups because of famine, warfare, pestilence, or governmental action. Many such groups are scattered along the Uganda side of the Uganda-Congo border because many people moved to flee from the harsh policies of the former Congo administration. This is a modern development, as before European administration prevented large-scale fighting such a group could not have settled in this way. Even today there is continual fighting along the Congo border, between Uganda Lugbara and families who try to settle from the Congo. The fighting involves only a few men and is sporadic because the government chiefs try to stop it. But the fighting and the bitterness that accompanies it are indicative of the values involved in the settlement of accessory groups: a group should come only when there are existing kinship ties, not try to take land belonging to others without entering into the full complex of kinship and neighborly behavior that is part of such a relationship. Those groups that have entered from the Congo are usually in fact allowed to remain, but people say of them, "They are new people; later we shall eat with them." In time, individuals intermarry, and later the immigrants will be assimilated and become accessory lineages proper of the groups on whose boundaries they live.

This type of movement, of an individual family going ahead to create ties and then being followed by others who attach themselves by these ties, is followed by Lugbara when emigrating as permanent settlers to Bunyoro and Buganda. They seem easily absorbed into the Buganda system, which is so structured that it can absorb culturally heterogenous elements into its chieftaincies (Richards 1956). In the areas where it occurs in Lugbara, mainly along the international boundaries, it is accompanied by much friction, expressed both in argument in and out of chiefs' courts and often in fighting to expel the "strangers who come to steal our land." This is in contrast to the general way in which "strangers" are welcomed and given land even when land is short, provided that there are already kinship ties in existence. The Lugbara system can absorb attached individuals, who may become the founders of later accessory groups, but it cannot easily absorb immigrant groups, with the one exception of the Ndu smiths, who are found throughout Lugbaraland; but these form an exception that does not disprove the generalization, inasmuch as they come as smiths and not as farmers. It is significant that their position is one surrounded by mystical sanctions of many kinds. The absorption of individuals means that they must be enmeshed in a network of kinship and neighborhood ties in order to lead any kind of social life. They cannot remain largely aloof as do the Lugbara immigrants in Bunyoro and Buganda. Even if they are culturally different— as are Kakwa who attach themselves to Lugbara hosts—they become Lugbara in culture as soon as they take up residence with their hosts. This type of attachment seems very much like that of Dinka in Nuer lineages, and of quite a different order from that of heterogeneous groups among neighboring peoples such as the Madi and Alur. Among both these peoples alien groups are absorbed partly by means of the institution of chiefship, which supplies a symbol of unity to groups of diverse origin, and which is lacking in Lugbara. Also the nature of the linking of component lineages within the subtribe is different, the Lugbara being very like the Nuer in this respect, but very different from the Madi and Alur (Middleton and Tait 1958; Evans-Pritchard 1940; Southall 1956).

Besides creating new ties between themselves and their host groups, the dispersal of attached groups and individuals widens the network of kinship ties of which their parent group is the center. An attached person maintains close ties with his parent lineage, since he is dependent upon its members ritually and in certain other ways, of which the most important is that his host will not make himself responsible for supplying the settler with bridewealth, most of which must come from his father. If he stays and founds a lineage these patrilineal ties become less and less recognized until after a generation or two they are forgotten.

Any genealogical account of a clan or lineage mentions movement of ancestors in the distant and semimythical past. Reference is made to the origin of groups that have moved elsewhere and are never visited. In this society a group twenty or thirty miles away is usually beyond visiting range, but generally visible across the open plateau. These traditions make sense of and give a pattern to the expanse of densely occupied country that is visible from any of the rocky outcrops that are scattered over the countryside and on which men take the air, women dry grain and clothes, and children play.

A lineage is named by the clan-name of the ancestors three or four generations back by whom it is differentiated from other lineages. If, for example, the founder of the lineage that is segmenting had two wives, the lineage will split into two, and each new segment will take as its new clan-name that of the wife from whom its members are directly descended. They thus recognize distant kin ties with the group from which that wife came before her marriage. Lineages bearing the same clan-name are thus linked either because they belong to the same clan, or because they are the "sisters' sons" of the group from which they have taken their name. These distant ties of clanship compose a network covering all Lugbara society and extend into neighboring societies. This was often the object of comment by my Lugbara companions. I was struck by the degree of hospitality, exemplified by the giving of food, beer, and labor to prepare the food, extended to us when we visited a group with which someone could establish kinship of this shadowy type. Also proper kinship terms were used. This was especially noticeable on the one or two occasions when the ties were those of patrilineal clanship, but sometimes we found ourselves among "mothers' brothers" of a range so distant as to be impossible to reckon; but it was said that it must exist and efforts were always made to find the tie by genealogical reckoning.

Remnant Clans

I have discussed the general process of clan segmentation as though clans and lineages invariably increase. But of course they sometimes dwindle in size, and die out. Members of a descent group that has decreased in numbers say "now we have all died, there are no people, we eat food by ourselves." The metaphor is that of ritual eating of food together, one of the basic norms of kinship. There are no related groups left to share sacrificial meat. Members of these groups say that they fear above all the destruction of their shrines, in which they place offerings for their ancestral ghosts, after the group has ceased to exist among the living. If this happens no one will place food for them in their turn and even the idea of the lineage will be extinguished. The shrines are taken by the lineage most closely related and placed in the grass away from the home-steads. The head of the caretaker lineage makes offerings as long as the livestock of the group that has died out remains. When the last member of the group is dead it is soon forgotten, even to its burial trees, which are the sole remaining signs of its existence.

There are many such groups that have dwindled to a few members. They are called "clans which remain," and I call them remnant clans. They consist of members who may be scattered over what was once their own territory but have become so reduced in numbers that the territory has been occupied by encroaching groups from other areas. Some of these remnant clans are still fairly large, with a few dozen members, but others today have only two or three old men waiting to die. There may be no sons and the daughters may have married elsewhere, or perhaps the sons have moved away to live with mothers' brothers because there is no longer any land or livestock for them to inherit. Such groups are found everywhere. They still have their own heads, but can never act as inde-pendent political units. Although so few in numbers, they still have full-length clan genealogies stretching back to the heroes. They are not important enough for other groups to know anything about their genealogies, but their own heads relate them at great length and point with pride to their burial trees as proof of their past.

The Lineage System

The inner workings of the subtribe and the subclan need some explana-tion. The Lugbara have what is called a segmentary lineage system. This means that they are organized into small groups that are regarded as being segments of larger groups. As segments they are distinct and their members think of themselves as forming separate groups in certain situations; but in other situa-tions they join together to form larger units. These larger units may in their turn join with other similar units to form still larger ones. At each level the units are thought of as equivalent. The total system is regarded as constant but the component groups are always changing; smaller groups may grow large and then segment to form two or more segments.

Lugbara conceive almost all social relations—certainly long-lasting ones —as operating within the framework of this system, and so one can understand little of their social life without a knowledge of it. A difficulty that faces the fieldworker in Lugbara is that they themselves cannot—or at least do not describe this system in abstract terms; they take it for granted. For the observer to make sense of it he must use several concepts (lineage, segment, section, and others) for which the Lugbara themselves have no specific terms. In this account I use the terms first used in this sense by Evans-Pritchard in his classic work on the Nuer (Evans-Pritchard 1940; see also Fortes and Evans-Pritchard 1940, and Middleton and Tait 1958).

The reader may well wonder why it is necessary for the anthropologist to use these special terms to describe a society whose members do not themselves find it necessary to do so. The anthropologist is sometimes accused of building up a needlessly complex structural model, while the people he is studying seem to manage very well without it. In the case of a people like the Lugbara the reason is simple, but I think it is important to state it. The Lugbara "live" their society; they do not have to describe it or analyze it so as to make sense of it to outsiders. For a Lugbara, the range of everyday social relations, the context of his everyday life, is narrow. He is concerned with at the most about a score of small local groups and lineages. He is brought up from childhood to know where they are on the ground and how their founding ancestors were related to one another. He has learned exactly how to behave to the members of these groups, and what to expect from them. He refers to them by their clan-names, or merely as "mother's brothers," "patrilineal kin," and so on. But the anthropologist is in a different position. He is, in a sense, outside and above the society. He moves from one part of the country to another and soon perceives that the organization of local groups is not haphazard but has a regular pattern. Most Lugbara are unaware of this because they do not travel far; they neither have to learn the internal organization of other groups, nor are they much interested in them. To describe this pattern, which is found throughout Lugbara, the anthropologist requires special terms which are not needed by the people themselves. But they can see the point of these terms when it is explained to them. I have found that when I described the over-all pattern to Lugbara, they saw it immediately, and were both pleased and, sometimes, surprised to learn that their own local organization was not unique to themselves but was found among all Lugbara.

Lugbara say that the basic units of their society are the sixty-or-so clans. As I have mentioned, the effective divisions of these clans today are the subclans. Apart from all Lugbaraland and the vaguely defined groups marked by differences of dialect or material culture, the largest local group is that formed around a subclan. I call this group a subtribe, and it consists of the men born into the subclan who have lived in the subtribe territory and not moved elsewhere, their wives and unmarried children, and various attached groups. Its structure is similar to that of the family cluster but on a larger scale: the family cluster includes about twenty-five people, the subtribe about four thousand. It is the largest group within which disputes and fighting must ultimately be settled by agreement—there cannot be a state of permanent warfare between units of one subtribe, but only between units of different subtribes.

A subtribe usually comprises between 150 and 200 family clusters, although many are smaller and many are larger than this. The family clusters are the largest groups, small as they are, with heads who have internal authority: these are the elders. Family clusters are grouped for certain purposes into larger units, which I call minor sections; minor sections are grouped into still larger ones, which I call major sections; and major sections join together to form subtribes. There may be more section levels, but these are typical. Most subtribes include from four to eight major sections, each comprising about twenty-five family clusters grouped into from two to four minor sections; each minor section has from two to ten family clusters. Obviously, these figures may vary, but what I have described is a typical subtribe.

Each of these levels of local grouping is concerned with various activities. The subtribe is the largest group within which disputes must ultimately be settled by agreement. The major section is—or was in the traditional system— the feuding unit. Within it disputes are settled by discussion or the operation of religious sanctions, because its members are regarded as too closely related by kinship for the exercise of force to be justifiable between them. At the lowest level the family cluster is the basic residential and political group. The minor section cannot be very clearly defined. It consists of several family clusters which have been until recently a single family cluster, and have recently segmented, so that ties of kinship are still extremely close between its members but they no longer recognize the authority of a single elder. This organization may be illustrated by a simple diagram:

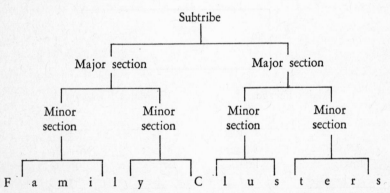

Here I have shown each group as consisting of only two segments of a lower order. In some cases a group has in fact only two segments, but it may have three, four, or as many as ten.

I have said that all descendants of the original clan founders have not remained in the original clan territories. Many have become dispersed and have attached themselves to host lineages in various parts of the country. A man may attach himself as sisters's son, sister's husband, or as a client, and his descendants then form an accessory lineage attached to that of his original host. The cluster of lineages thus formed is a section. A section does not always contain accessory lineages, but at least it always includes its members' wives, who are not members of their husbands' lineages, by the rule of clan exogamy.

A section is a local group composed of people living in families: they are real people living on the ground. But a lineage, as Lugbara conceive it, is a descent group, consisting of both ancestors and their living descendants: one cannot see a lineage, although one can see those members of it who are alive at the present time. Lineage unity is an important value. Thus women born into a lineage and married elsewhere return home from time to time, especially on the occasion of sacrifice to their ancestors by the lineage elders. Certain rights are vested in lineages, the principal ones being those in the resources of land, livestock, and women. Their living members act together in certain situations, such as those of marriage, ritual, fighting and feud, and dancing at funerals. Many of the living members of a lineage are likely to be living in different sections, but they are still thought of as composing a corporate group in which certain rights are vested. This group is thought of by Lugbara as permanent, whereas they know that a section may form and disband in time.

To understand how this system works the social anthropologist has to make this distinction between lineage and section. But the Lugbara do not do so in everyday speech. A section is merely given the name of its host lineage. A lineage system therefore reflects the system of sections (see diagram on page 37), and provides for Lugbara the idiom in which the section system is conceived:

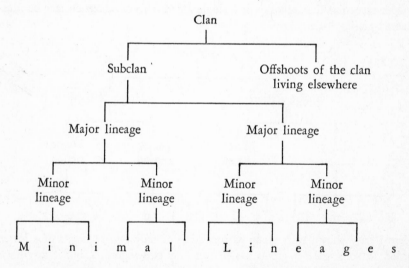

Every lineage, of whatever size, has a founder whose name is remembered by his living descendants. In this way a genealogy preserves the memory of the ancestors and also charts the distribution of the component lineages of any sub-clan. At the same time it indicates the distribution on the ground of the various sections that are associated with these lineages.

This system enables the Lugbara to think of their society, and particularly of their own subtribe, as having some kind of order and stability. In fact, the family clusters that compose the subtribe are always moving about in search of new fields and hut sites. Some may die out, others may increase in number and segment into new family clusters; others may attach themselves to lineages elsewhere as accessory groups. Lugbara make sense of this fluid situation by thinking of it in terms of lineage and genealogy. Whether or not a man moves from one part of the subtribe territory to another, his status in the lineage and his position in its genealogy remain fixed. Also, the continuity of lineages through time, as corporate groups, is thought of in the same way. Due to demographic, ecological, and other factors the system of sections is in constant change, but the system of lineages is seen as permanent, or at least as relatively so. By reference to it Lugbara can see their society as coherent and stable.

Lugbara have generic names for these groups, the words *ori'ba* and *suru*. *Ori'ba* means "ghost people"—*ori* is the ghost of an ancestor for whom a shrine has been built by his descendants—and consists of a group of people who share common ghost shrines. *Ori'ba* are primarily those groups under the ritual authority of an elder. They are typically minimal and minor lineages and sections.

Suru has the meaning of a group of people who consider themselves and are considered by others to form a group because they share a territory and have ties between them based on common ancestry. The ritual content of the ties that bind members of an *ori'ba* is absent. Thus *suru* refers to major lineages and sections, clans, subclans, and subtribes. The term is used also in a wider sense as the *suru* (peoples, tribes) of Madi or Europeans, and as "species" or "category," as in a *suru* of birds or trees. This is not to say that Lugbara see birds and trees as organized into lineages—although since all creatures are descended from those put in Meme's womb by the Creator Spirit there is something of this idea present, and cattle are definitely classed by lines of descent from ancestral cattle whose names are remembered—but as being differentiated from other creatures with different characteristics.

Rainmakers and Holders of Political Authority

It is convenient at this point to say something about holders of authority outside the family cluster.

The Lugbara have no king, nor do they possess traditional chiefs. The head of the minimal lineage holds domestic authority over all members of his family cluster. Those elders who are also genealogically the heads of minor and major lineages have no domestic authority over any but their own family clusters, but they may act as representatives of the minor or major lineages on ritual occasions. They are still called only elders. They may wield very considerable influence by virtue of their position but they may not be superior in internal authority to genealogically junior elders of the same lineage. A fairly senior man said of one extremely respected elder, the genealogical head of a major lineage: "We fear the words of Maro. He speaks slowly and is never angry or quarrelsome. Truly he is an elder and we little men follow his words. He leads us like a bull leads his herd of cattle." But when I asked whether Maro would intervene in a dispute in a family cluster other than his own, I was told, "He is the elder of that lineage there, and we do not listen to what he says. Here our elder is Draa and we follow him." This elder's influence was considerable enough for the local county chief to ask for his opinions and heed them, but it did not extend to the internal affairs of lineages other than his own minimal lineage.

There are traditionally certain other functionaries who exercise some political authority in Lugbara. Besides the elders there are men called *opi*, the word used today also for county chiefs in the system of government-appointed chiefs. *Opi* are strongest in northern Lugbara, persumably because this is the longest settled area and southern Lugbara is largely occupied by small dispersed groups who have moved there from the north; important men and their lineages are less likely to move than poorer men. (It is noticeable that there are fewer traditional ritual specialists in the south than in the north.) Information about the *opi* is confused. Their traditional powers have been taken from them, and there is still much bitterness about the way in which some of the lesser ones were made chiefs by the Belgians, with powers quite beyond anything they originally possessed, while the "true" *opi* were ignored. Members of the lineages of those made chiefs by the Belgians, having inherited the position, exaggerate the traditional powers of the *opi* to make them equal to those of the chiefs today. Other government chiefs and those traditional *opi* who have not been given administrative powers denigrate each other and minimize the others' powers. During my stay, for example, there was considerable unrest in one area of northern Lugbara due to the amalgamation of the territories of certain of these functionaries, a consequence of which was that the power of the government chiefs was further increased at the expense of the traditional *opi*, whose existence and affiliations were ignored. There was fighting, and feeling against the government ran very high. The traditional *opi* were almost in hiding and were gathering support for their traditional powers, while the government chiefs did not dare to go into these areas. During my stay also the colonial administration introduced the practice of having subcounty chiefs elected instead of being appointed by chiefs. The consequence was the heavy defeat of certain candidates who were sons of county chiefs, and commoners were elected in their place.

There are various indigenous functionaries called *opi*, all with rudimentary political authority. The most important, today at any rate, are the rainmaker chiefs, *opi-ezo*, ("chiefs of rain"). The power to make and control rain is thought to run in certain descent lines and is usually limited to one such line in a subclan. It is usually, but not always, the genealogically senior descent line. Inheritance of the power is limited to the rainmaker's own minimal lineage, and this is so important that if a rainmaker has no sons but only daughters the power may be inherited through the eldest daughter to her son, who is adopted into her natal lineage for the purpose. Rainmaking power is held by the custodian of certain sacred objects—rainstones, obsidian necklaces, and iron hoes of a peculiar type[2]—handed down from the earliest ancestors who received them from the Creator Spirit. Rain is made by the manipulation of the rainstones, which are kept in oil-filled pots hidden in rain groves.

Rainmakers have other roles besides that of controlling rain, although most of them are no longer important. A man who was the victim of a quarrel could go to the rainmaker and clasp his feet. He was then under the protection of the rainmaker, who would summon the elders of the persons concerned and discuss the matter. He could administer poison ordeals and forbid continuance of the offense. The person adjudged guilty is said to have given a bull to the rainmaker. A rainmaker had the power to forbid fighting between lineages of the same subtribe, by the exercise of his curse. He had the power to try suspected witches and persistent evildoers by ordeal, involving the eating of earth from the grave of a man whose death had been caused by the suspect. He could purify men who had killed opponents in fighting. The general respect paid to him is extreme—especially when contrasted to the general lack of overt respect paid by Lugbara to anyone in authority over them, in particular to government-appointed chiefs—and his person may not be touched in anger without incurring mystical penalties.

There are also *opi* called *'ba rukuza* ("men whose names are known"). They have secular powers rather than ritual ones. They are well-known and wealthy men, who have many clients and followers. They do not transmit the title to their descendants. In the past they wielded very considerable power and influence and are said to have arbitrated in disputes as did rainmakers. But they had no formal authority and no religious sanctions for their power. "They are like mahogany trees in the forest, they support and give strength to everyone," it is said of them. They are said to have carried special white spears or staves as marks of rank. At times of famine people would come from great distances to attach themselves to them as clients in return for food and assistance. There were also temporary war leaders, the status, a very informal one, being dependent on individual prowess and ability.

'Ba rukuza are found mainly in northern Lugbara. In that area also are men called *adro'ba* ("spirit-men"), who have the power to utter curses against persistent evildoers. Formerly they walked with a spear and a bundle of arrows, with a special armlet. Both they and the *'ba rukuza* are scattered throughout subtribes and sections irrespective of the distribution of descent groups. On the other hand, there is usually only one rainmaker in each subclan, his status depending upon genealogical position rather than on individual personal qualities.

Rainmakers are ritual functionaries who have or had certain political and judicial roles associated with their ritual attributes. It is probable that the institution was borrowed from the Kakwa to the north and the Madi to the east,

---

[2] Rainstones are either of quartz (*si,* the word used also for hail, both quartz and hail thought of as falling from the sky) or granite, and are "male" and "female." There is no obsidian in Lugbara, and I do not know the source of the necklaces. The hoes are similar to those used by the Bari-speaking groups to the north.

both of whom have similar functionaries but with considerably more powers than in Lugbara, and in both cases separate from secular functionaries. The *'ba rukuza* and *adro'ba* may have arisen primarily as a response to outside Arab, European, and other tribal contacts. At least it may be said that these contacts increased their importance. Many of the *'ba rukuza* had influence over very large areas, especially in the north and northeast, the only parts of Lugbara subjected to prolonged outside contact. As I have said earlier, some of them were made chiefs by the Belgians because they were the only men with any obvious influence extending over wide areas, and later they, their brothers, sons, or sisters' sons were made chiefs under the British. None were rainmakers. They were not found, so far as I know, in southern Lugbara. In general the relationship between government chiefs and rainmakers is unfriendly. The latter see the former as upstarts and "Europeans," and I have been told that "To say we are big men and brothers, like these county and subcounty chiefs do now, is bad; *opi* do not do that."

4

The Wider Community

Interlineage Relations and Law and Order

THE LUGBARA TRADITIONALLY LACK any form of kingship or even chief-ship. They also lack any clearly formulated law. There were, traditionally, neither courts nor machinery for enforcing legal decisions made in the light of codified jural offenses and punishments. It is sometimes said that members of societies such as this depend upon self-help to enable them to right their wrongs and maintain social order. Yet clearly uncontrolled self-help would lead to anarchy. Lugbara say that the exercise of both authority and power are essential for the orderly operation of their society. The exercise of power alone is a sign of lack of close social relationships, whereas that of authority, which is both legitimate and responsible, is what distinguishes them from both the mythical figures at the beginning of the world and those "inverted" people living beyond the fringes of their world. All legitimate authority is controlled by the ancestors, who originated orderly social life. They control relations within the local community, and use mainly religious sanctions to that end. When these break down between people who do not recognize the same recent ancestors, then self-help becomes the only means of keeping order, but even so, it is subject to various controls that prevent it from erupting into mere anarchic violence.

Everyday life for Lugbara is concerned with growing crops, attending markets and dances, meeting kin, friends, and neighbors and eating, drinking, and talking with them, and marriage and courtship. Formerly an important activity was fighting, and today its place has been taken by attendance at and discussion about cases dealt with at the courts of government-appointed chiefs. Most of these activities are shared with one's neighbors, the members of one's local community. I have met many old Lugbara who have never been more than ten miles from the compound in which they were born, but I have met others with the most amazing history of traveling. Traditionally there was a certain amount of contact over long distances, with trading expeditions, groups attending

43

the death dances of distant kinsmen, and traveling for food in times of periodic famines. Today there is much traveling about. Young men will walk many miles to visit their girls, and most of them go outside Lugbaraland altogether to work in southern Uganda for a period to earn money for taxes and bridewealth. But in general, and for most people, nearly all everyday activities take place within a small neighborhood a few miles across and never very far from one's own homestead—and almost always within sight of it. A woman changes her home at marriage and therefore is a member of two small neighborhoods; but they are usually close enough together to permit regular visiting.

The formalized relations of everyday life—such as those having to do with marriage—are conceived in terms of categories of kin, which I discuss below, but other relations may not be so conceived. People say that they go to trade with "the people of such and such a place." All places in the country are named. The territories of sections and subtribes are named after the lineages and subclans which occupy them as hosts, and hills, valleys, outcrops of rock, streams, clumps of trees and single trees, even if not burial trees, may all have names. Thus in situations in which lineage ties are not primarily significant these names of places are used to refer to the people concerned. People do not attend markets, for example, as members of lineage groups as such. The women of a kin group may walk to market together, and if selling may set out their goods on the ground together, but this is incidental to the exchange of goods between individuals. Although the situation is permeated by kinship considerations—a woman may give better terms to a kinswoman than to a stranger—lineage ties are not significant in the main activity. Here, and in many other situations, such as the watching of death dances, which always attract large crowds of neighbors, people tend to stand and talk and drink according to lineage affiliation, but this affiliation is not primarily significant. It is merely that kinsmen, close friends, and neighbors tend to be the same people. Lineage ties are so all-embracing that it is sometimes difficult to distinguish formalized lineage ties from unformalized ties. The distinction lies mainly in the sanctions underlying them, that is, whether or not the ancestors and their ghosts are involved.

Before discussing the nature of relations between lineages and sections of varying span, I mention two important concepts used by Lugbara. I have described the formal structure of sections and lineages in terms of which relations between them are conceived. This is a formal structure, a paradigm by which Lugbara comprehend their society as having consistency and permanence both in space and time. Local groups are small in numbers and in size, and with the high density of population the political relations of a given family cluster cover a considerable number of other groups—agnatically related, related through uterine kinship, ties of clientship, ties of clanship, and so on. The hopeless confusion in which the observer finds himself after a few month of study of Lugbara local groups is inevitable when trying to sort out the composition and interrelationships of these myriad little clusters of people. The system of lineages is continually changing, as they change in size, segment, or merge with others. The names of the lineages with which people come into contact are never likely to be the same for very long. Lugbara, like anyone else, would seem to need to imagine their society as stable, and to ignore the continual changing in the pattern of groups around them on the ground. They can do this by the use of certain categories which refer to social distance.

At the center of a man's social life is his homestead, and beyond that the homesteads of his family cluster. Beyond that lie the homesteads of his *o'dipi* and *juru*. I cannot find suitable English translations for these terms, and shall have to ask the reader to accept the Lugbara terms. *O'dipi* comprise those groups that are related patrilineally, but including also others near them, such as sisters' sons living in the same family cluster. The range of *o'dipi* and their composition vary in different situations, sometimes being close patrilineal kin only, sometimes close patrilineal kin and attached uterine kin, and sometimes including distant patrilineal kin. Beyond the range of *o'dipi* are the *juru*. *Juru* and *o'dipi* together comprise all those groups with which a person, as a member of a family cluster, has direct social relations, although the further limits of *juru* cannot be very clearly demarcated. *Juru* do not stretch away to the ends of the earth, but are people who, though unrelated by kinship or whose kin-relationship is irrelevant on a given occasion, are nevertheless in a social relationship. In the context of fighting, one fights with arrows against *juru* and not against *o'dipi;* in that of exogamy, one marries *juru* and not *o'dipi*. In these two cases the range of *o'dipi* varies; one may fight people whom one cannot marry because they are too closely related. Territorially some *juru* will be closer than some *o'dipi,* but socially they are more distant. They are conceptual categories and not groups, although, of course, they have reference to groups.

Juru thus extend to the limits of social relations. At the limit of *juru* are those groups with which there are indirect social relations, such as distant kin of people with whom one is in a state of feud. It may be said, more or less, that the limits of a group's *juru* coincide with the range of sorcerers and magicians, in the scheme of sociospatial categories mentioned in Chapter 2; but Lugbara do not usually put the two sets of concepts into a single scheme of thought.

By the use of these concepts Lugbara can avoid inconsistency and contradiction by using terms applied according to situation rather than to span or genealogical depth.

Juru are essentially groups between which any religious sanction is lacking. In actual situations involving the threat of force—the only sanction where religious sanctions are not operative—it is actual sections and lineages that are concerned. The relationship of *juru* must be translated, as it were, into that between local groups as they are on the ground. The subjectively defined and relative *juru* are composed of objectively defined sections and lineages. The former are units in the conceptual scheme, the latter units in the actual political system. Political relations are those that are ultimately settled by the use of socially approved force, that is, they are concerned with conflicts of interests between groups that can be settled only by fighting. Within the smaller groups fighting does not occur, because ties of kinship are stronger and religious sanctions become operative. The point at which these kinship ties become too weak to prohibit fighting varies from one subtribe to another. Like every situation in Lugbara, it is relative. Political relations shade into those that are not political.

Feud and Warfare

Lugbara society is in a constant state of instability, which arises from conflict of interests between groups and persons. There are several ways in which these conflicts can be controlled. One is by the various institutions that prevent or at least mitigate open hostility. These include the recognition of lineage ties between units likely to be in conflict, so that open hostility becomes a breach of lineage and kinship ties. Another way is by blood compensation, so that fighting once started can at least be stopped without prolonging it for vengeance. Still another way of controlling conflicts is by calling into operation various legal, religious, and other sanctions.

It is an old anthropological hypothesis that the significance of an offense is defined not only by its intrinsic nature, nor by its motive, but by the social distance between the parties concerned. This holds good for the Lugbara. Here I am referring to the traditional system. Since the coming of the European administration there has developed a new category of offenses which are offenses because of their intrinsic nature—tax evasion, refusal to carry chiefs' baggage, attend sleeping-sickness inspections, cut grass for sleeping-sickness clearance, supply grain and build granaries for famine reserves, and so on. Admittedly when they are considered before chiefs' courts the relationship of offender to chief may not be entirely irrelevant, but on the whole offenses are judged on their merits, the main aim of the administration in this sphere. Also, chiefs have been appointed who are outside the traditional system of authority altogether, with the power to use force of a type previously unknown. Judgment and the means of enforcing it has little or nothing to do with the status of the offender. On the other hand, traditionally, the status of an offender was strictly relevant to the response against him for his offense, since only certain kinds of force could in fact be brought to bear upon him by the local community. These were violence, various types of mystical sickness believed to be sent in various ways, ostracism, banishment, and occasionally mutilation or severe beating, sometimes to death, by members of the local community. The approval of at least a fair proportion of community members was needed before any of these could be made effective. Lugbara see most ties between members of a community in terms of kinship, and because one of the most sacred duties of kinship is support for a fellow kinsman in his troubles, it was not always easy to acquire sufficient support, by an individual or a group, to control an offender.

I have been using the past tense. Except for certain types of violence these traditional sanctions are still used, and traditional offenses that called them into operation still occur. I shall use the present tense, even when referring to violence which is now prohibited by the government. In the Lugbara society, the system of administration, operated by officers of the central government and the district local government (including the chiefs) is found side by side with the traditional organization. Every individual feels the indirect effects of administration, but it is only the heads of families who are directly concerned with its agents, the chiefs and headmen. The remainder of the population spend their lives without ever being directly and personally concerned with the newly imposed system.[1] This system cannot be ignored in a discussion of the Lugbara of today; but it does not affect every aspect of life, and we are here concerned with a system that has so far changed very little and in which the traditional and imposed elements may fairly clearly be distinguished.

Disputes in Lugbara are about the distribution and enjoyment of rights over the resources of land, livestock, and women, and about the maintenance, abuse, or usurpation of status and authority, both of the living and of the dead. They are expected in the history of development of any lineage. It is in the nature of things for lineages to proliferate, segment, amalgamate with others, and even die out. These processes are given meaning and expressed in terms of disputes between their members, just as migrations of clans are told in terms of the wanderings of individual ancestors who quarreled among themselves. Fighting is an important social activity, as the myths of the heroes make plain. Lugbara do not analyze their disputes and their underlying causes any more than we usually do. Like ourselves, they see them generally as arising from the disagreement of quarrelsome individuals and from the apparent anarchy of everyday life. But a more careful analysis can produce a more meaningful pattern.

Lugbara have never fought wars of conquest. Warfare against Kakwa, Madi, and other neighboring peoples seems to have been due mainly to pressure of population and the need for new land by border subtribes, and was of the same order as warfare between subtribes within the boundaries of Lugbaraland. Because families on the borders marry across them, disputes were often over bridewealth transfers, as among Lugbara themselves, and the fighting seems to have been no more brutal or prolonged than within Lugbaraland.

The most valuable resource in the country is land. Every household is dependent upon the use of the various types of land I have mentioned earlier, and any wife who cannot get adequate fields complains to her husband. There is constant bickering between wives of a family cluster over the allocation of fields. Allocation is difficult, since provision must be made for each field-type, grazing, and such resources as firewood, trees, water, and even granite outcrops for drying grain and cassava. A woman whose compound is farther from water or rocky outcrops than those of other wives complains that if her fields were only better sited she would have an easier time and could work better in her fields. Demands for land, wealth, respect, and so on, all lead to the building-up of tensions. How these are expressed and which set of demands is given precedence depends on factors such as the richness or poverty of soil or grazing, the abundance or

---

[1] There are some exceptions which are becoming more important. One is the need to vote for chiefs and members of political parties, which was only in the first stages during my stay. And the other, of course, is the need for younger men to work as labor migrants for a period.

scarcity of water, reeds, clay, and so on, and also on personality. Lugbara recognize that some people are better-tempered than others, that some are greedy, some are aggressive, others are gentle, and others lazy.

Land becomes scarce through increase in population and decrease in soil fertility, the former being the more important. In the past, lineages would fight against one another for land, beginning with skirmishing between individuals as a consequence of trespass, such as the grazing or clearing of another group's fallow fields. The other most common reason for fighting between groups is that of a wife who runs away from her husband. Her group usually refuses to return the bridewealth or returns only a portion of it. Then either the husband's group captures one of her lineage as a hostage to be killed if the bridewealth is not repaid, or the husband takes some of her family livestock in reparation. Other common reasons are the seduction of a girl followed by refusal to pay the seduction fine, adultery, drunken quarrels and assault, accusations of witchcraft, and quarrels arising from oracular sessions and the theft of livestock without cause. Lugbara say that women are "evil," causing strife and trouble to everyone who comes into contact with them. The high proportion of disputes over women is shown by the proportion of cases brought to chiefs' courts today. Because fighting is now prohibited, cases which in the past would have led to fighting come to the chiefs, and most cases in courts involve women. Other cases are still settled in traditional ways not involving fighting. Disputes resulting in cases being taken to chiefs' courts are more prevalent among groups living at a high density and suffering from considerable land shortage. Also it much depends upon the personality of the local chief or subchief whether people take cases to him at all; some disputes that would once have been settled by fighting may not come to a chief in one area but will be taken to court in another.

Lugbara talk about fighting nostalgically and at length, as an example of the ideal life in the happy days now gone as a consequence of the "words of the Europeans." Today fighting is forbidden by the government. It still breaks out but is quickly stopped by the chiefs and rarely spreads to other than the immediate families of the individuals involved. But all men over middle age and many younger men have taken part in proper fighting—up to the late 1920s— and their information would seem to be reliable, although perhaps prone to excited exaggeration when describing fighting in which the speaker's own lineage was involved.

The weapons used by Lugbara are arrows, spears, and clubs. The arrows are headed and barbed, and often smeared with the poisonous juice of the euphorbia tree. They can be shot accurately up to about thirty yards. Spears are about four feet long, with blades about a foot long. They can be thrown but are usually used in close combat and can give serious wounds. Clubs are of many kinds, all being of wood and often studded with pieces of metal. Most Lugbara fighting was between small groups of men who would creep up to their enemy and shoot off a volley of arrows. Once the element of surprise was lost they would stand in lines and shoot more arrows, then close in for spear fighting. Although old men give the impression that fights lasted days and even weeks and involved whole major sections and even subtribes, it is clear that they were sporadic, and were the immediate concern of only a few men at any one time. Also killing and even serious wounding was not all that common. The shouting of abuse was often as important a way of letting off steam as actual wounding and killing.

A group would not fight with arrows and spears against members of the same minor lineage, or in some cases of the same major lineage, the group called *ori'ba*. Its being called *ori'ba* ("ghost people") shows that within it relations are sanctioned by the ghosts and by mystical sanctions rather than by open force exercised by living members. Quarrels within this group are with fists and sticks only. They arise for personal reasons and are stopped by the elders or by on-lookers. When women fight, by striking their combatants' mouths with the sides of their hands and by pulling their hair, kicking, and biting, it is the duty of their husbands and brothers to stop them. These fights are always individual and personal, and are quite different from intergroup fighting with weapons, which is traditionally the activity of men.

A group fought with weapons against other groups which it called *juru,* those outside the major section. *Juru* does not mean "enemy" but refers to those groups which may be fought with weapons. When the groups actually fought, they became *ari'ba* ("blood men").

A man killed by a member of his own major section, but of a different minor section, was avenged by the killing of any man of his minor section. If the victim were of a more distant relationship to the killer, retaliation would be made on a member of his major section. Retaliation was made at night. "They came upon our people at night 'like a bomb.' How could they know whether they chose to kill a host member or a stranger attached to that lineage?" an informant said to me when relating the history of past feuds of his lineage. He said:

> When you walked among *juru* you did not fear. They did not kill you on sight. They said, "Perhaps this man comes to see our sisters and to sleep with them; he does no ill." If your lineage lost a man or woman who had gone to visit another lineage, if he did not return, you went to look for him. Then slowly you heard they had killed him. Then at night you went to kill those people; men of your lineage without counting went there to kill as many as they could. They came back, having killed many, perhaps five, perhaps ten. They came here to fight, the enemies closed their hearts to die. The elder consulted his rat oracle, perhaps his chicken oracle, to see whether they would be successful. Now it was fighting (*adi*) and it did not stop. People entered secretly to kill. Then the elders tired of these things and slowly they went to mend words among themselves.

Such fighting might last a week or a month, but apparently rarely longer, although it might break out again on a later occasion without much provocation. There were no set times in the year for fighting: "Could you choose when people come to kill you?" I was asked. But it was unlikely for fighting to continue over the times of clearing fields, planting, or harvesting.

Most intergroup fighting was over women. Therefore it was relatively uncommon among patrilineally related lineages between which marriage is forbidden. *Juru* in this context included groups related to a minimal lineage, as one of its member's wife's kin, since it was usually among affines that fighting over women started. The distinction is here clear between intergroup and interpersonal ties. In fighting as a member of his lineage against a lineage in which he, as an individual, had ties of maternal or affinal kinship, a man would try not to shoot arrows at his own kinsmen. He would shout at them to stand aside but if they did not do so loyalty to his own lineage would prevail and he might shoot them. I know of a few men who found themselves in this position. They had to go to their dead kinsman's home to mourn his death. There such a visitor could not be killed since the killers would have died "of his blood," but they tried to kill him for vengeance on the way back once they had left their territory or later if they avenged the death. Also such a man was liable to a much feared curse from his mother, who would take off her pubic leaves and throw them at her son, saying: "I bore you and now you kill my brother." As a lineage member a man had to fight on the side of his "brothers" but tried not to harm his own maternal or affinal kinsman; but his half-brothers might kill his mother's kin, and "brothers" by different fathers might kill his affines, since they did not themselves have the same ties.

Fighting among groups of the same subtribe could be stopped by the joint efforts of the elders directly concerned, who could curse any of their dependants who continued to fight. They could also put a future curse on anyone who quarreled over certain common rights, such as that of drawing water from a stream between two groups, or walking through a neighboring group to death dances and other rites. These were operative only within the subtribe, which is based upon the subclan. Bonds of common ancestry were invoked to prohibit further fighting, the antithesis of such relationship. There was no set mechanism for the elders to talk peacefully. They merely let it be known that they thought continued fighting pointless. Often mutual sisters' sons would act as intermediaries, and women were also so used, often being killed while acting in this capacity. If, however, the fighting groups belonged to different subtribes it is said that the groups continued to fight until the matter was settled and forgotten, after an equal number of persons had been killed on each side. But in any case fighting would give way to necessary economic activity, whether the dispute were settled or not. Subtribal territories were surrounded by land used for grazing and for distant millet fields under shifting cultivation, and much fighting consisted of raids across this land. If one party decided to put down their weapons and go out with hoes and axes to cultivate, the other side would not attack them. "We would see those people were without bows; they carried hoes and went to cultivate. Then we would know 'they have tired of the fighting and wished to cultivate because perhaps the time is here and the rains are here.' Then we would also hoe. And later we would forget that fighting." The need to hoe was used as an excuse to draw fighting to a close without losing face.

In northern Lugbara fighting within the subtribe could be stopped by the rainmaker chief. He called people together after a lull in the fighting, wearing a cattleskin, and forbade further strife. His words carried the force of a curse, and in some localities it is said that his person was sanctuary for an evildoer, whose case would be put to arbitration by the rainmaker rather than closed by his summary killing.

Following ordinary anthropological usage, we may refer to fighting within the subtribe as feud, and to that between subtribes as warfare. The essential difference is that there was the obligation to settle feuds by peaceful means, whereas there was no such obligation in the case of warfare.

Fighting did not, however, always occur in response to disputes, even in response to homicide. The reaction to this offense is always crucial to the understanding of any judicial system, and in Lugbara it throws a good deal of light on the nature of formal hostility and the structure of the lineage and subclan. There is no social response in terms of force for homicide within the minimal lineage. It is a sin for which there is no humanly awarded punishment. I knew a man who killed his father's brother's son, a "brother" of the same minimal lineage, thinking that he had speared a witch in the guise of a leopard that had been following him. He was drunk at the time and when sober went to the government subchief and confessed to what he had done. When I asked what would happen to him, people said: "There are no words. Who will help him now his brother is dead? He will bewail him alone, and die of his brother's blood." A bull was paid on his behalf by his elder (he himself was sent to prison) to his dead "brother's" mother's brother and he inherited his widows. Traditionally nothing further could have happened, because the death could not be avenged. The usual cleansing rites for a homicide do not apply to a fratricide, who commits a deed that is unthinkable and that could never be done deliberately. People say of him, "he is like a *juru*" and fear and avoid him as unnatural; he has broken all bonds of kinship. The beast paid to the victim's mother's brother is not blood money. It is known as "the beast to give (for) the corpse." It is eaten by the group receiving it and not placed in their herd: "Our sister's son would have lived and begotten children, but now his days are cut."

If a fight within the same major lineage leads to death the killer gives compensation of two bulls and two cows to the victim's sons, "for them to get wives with," and one bull is also given to his mother's brother.

Beyond the major lineage and section no blood money is payable. Retaliation is made and the situation is of a different order. Close kinship ties are here irrelevant and can be forgotten. A man who killed an enemy—not a mere homicide, but a killing in feud—outside his own major section formally and ceremonially rejoiced and was ritually cleansed by his elder. If it were not done the killer died of "blood" due to the victim's anger, because at this range compensation is not given. Traditionally, if the victim were of a group "far away," that is, of another subtribe, his penis and his right thumb ("with which he shoots people") were cut off and his corpse left to be collected by the girls of his lineage, who would not be molested. These parts were placed on a tree, "spiked like (sacrificial) meat" on a branch, and his head was sometimes placed on the path by which he had come. "Truly he was a man, but now we have conquered him." Sometimes penis and thumb were placed in the bundles of sticks called *siriba,* bundles of great magical power kept in the thatch of the owner's hut. It is said that the victim's heart was also removed and eaten by the killer's lineage. Lugbara do not pride themselves on having been noble fighters—if a man could kill an enemy by stealth and guile he did so. In the accounts I have been given, the details of mutilating the corpse and jeering at the discomforted foes are always told with great glee, and clearly this aspect was considered extremely important, as it was the point at which intergroup hostility was realized to its fullest extent.

Chiefs, Headmen, and the Administration of Justice

Although the Lugbara had no chiefs before the advent of colonial government, today the chiefs are important people and an integral part of Lugbara society. The first chiefs appointed were meant to administer subtribes. But these units were too small to be politically independent and they were amalgamated into counties and subcounties at various times between 1920 and 1950. By 1950 most larger subtribes were administered by subcounty chiefs, and the smaller ones were part of subcounties. By 1950, county and subcounty chiefs were educated men, each with an office, tiled brick house, court and small jail, and with a few police, clerks, and other petty officials. They were members of a local bureaucracy, usually without ties of lineage with the people whom they administered. Up to about 1945 many of the older chiefs had been men from their own chiefdoms; most had been illiterate, and although much respected were unable to cope with many of the problems of modern administration. They were retired and more educated men appointed in their places. At the time I was in Lugbaraland, county and subcounty chiefs were paid career officials, as were the members of their staffs.

Beneath them are parish chiefs[2] and headmen. They are paid only very small salaries, are mostly illiterate and uneducated, and are not regarded as "chiefs" by the Lugbara. Parish chiefs are usually responsible for major sections or the smaller subtribes, and headmen are responsible for minor and sometimes major sections. They are almost always drawn from the areas they represent. They have neither courts, offices, nor staff; they do, however, hold informal meetings, which I call moots.

Certain offenses, as I have mentioned, are regarded as criminal offenses and dealt with by a subchief's summons and a hearing at his court, from which appeal may be made to a county chief's court. The most prevalent of these offenses is tax evasion. Homicide and rape are also considered criminal offenses today. Civil offenses, arising from disputes between individuals, are treated

---

[2] The term "parish" has been used in Uganda for a small administrative unit, and lacks the religious connotation of the English "parish."

I have written about modern Lugbara chiefs and headmen elsewhere (Middleton 1960a) and here present only an outline account.

somewhat differently. If the parties to the dispute are both within the small group administered by a headman or a parish chief they usually take it to a moot. Headmen and parish chiefs have no means to enforce a decision, but merely bring the dispute into the open and use their powers of persuasion to resolve it and restore peace and friendship. A moot is informal and attended by those who care to do so: these are usually older men and those known for their wisdom and knowledge of Lugbara tradition and precedent. The aim of a moot is not to punish but to restore neighborhood ties which have been disrupted by quarrels. If the moot cannot do this, the case will be taken to the subchief's court. There the subchief can give verdicts involving punishments of imprisonment, fines, or compensation.

But if the disputants are under the authority of different parish chiefs the case goes directly to a subchief's court. In this case each party will first discuss the matter with his own parish chief who goes with him to the court as a sponsor. The parish chief may often plead for him before the subchief. The subchief is impartial, both because he does not have ties of kinship or lineage with the parties before him, and because the Lugbara regard county and subcounty chiefs as representatives of the central government rather than of themselves; they see them as *Mundu* ("Europeans"), members of the class known as "New People," rather than as "one of us."

It is noticeable that the chiefs' courts deal with those disputes that would in the past have been settled by fighting. Disputes that were traditionally settled by peaceful means are nowadays dealt with either by elders (if the parties are closely related) or by headmen (if they are just neighbors). From figures which I collected from various subchiefs' court records I found that about 40 percent were in respect to seduction of unmarried girls; about 30 percent were brought by the chiefs themselves for tax evasion or failure to carry out government orders; about 15 percent were for assault, usually arising from marital disputes. In short, chiefship today has taken over the role formerly played by feud and warfare.

5

Marriage and Maternal Kinship

Marriage and Exogamy

INTERGROUP FIGHTING is intimately connected with relations based on marriage as it is the only sanction for orderly relations between lineages not related by kinship. The myths of the heroes show this connection, and Lugbara themselves state it quite explicitly.

Marriage in Lugbara is marked by the transfer of bridewealth from the minimal lineage of the bridegroom to that of the bride. By the rules of exogamy that regulate the choice of a wife, a man may not marry a girl of his own clan. Nor may he marry into the major lineage of his mother; this prohibition is inherited for three generations.

The range of permitted marriage is not the same as that of permitted sexual relations. This may be seen particularly on occasions such as death dances, when young men may openly say that they have intercourse with distant clan sisters. This intercourse, which is considered rather dashing by the young men concerned, takes place outside the compounds, in the grassland, and must not be followed by conception. If the girl becomes pregnant, the two are considered to have committed incest, a serious offense which needs ritual purification. A man would not have intercourse with a distant clan sister inside her hut, however, as this would be tampering with the rights held in her by her father. And he would not marry her.

The traditional pattern of courtship is for girls to be visited by young men in the special girls' hut built at the edge of the compound of a family cluster. This hut is under the care of an old widow of the lineage, and in it sleep the girls and young men. An adolescent girl is visited by as many boys as she cares to accept. To accept the same boy too often is considered "greedy" and is ridiculed. The boys enter the hut at dusk and leave before dawn. Usually sets of brothers visit sets of sisters. Physical intercourse is not permitted. It is traditionally regarded as a form of rape, the boy being beaten by the girl's brothers and even put to death. Today, however, intercourse is common,[1] and a seduction fine of a bull is paid only if the girl becomes pregnant. By the time the girl is about fourteen years old she has decided whom she wishes to marry. The father of the young man consults the elder and other senior men of the minimal lineage. If there are no bars of exogamy, the elder goes to discuss the matter with the girl's elder. This leads to much visiting, during which both sides are perfectly aware of the reasons for this calling, although the actual marriage negotiations may not be opened for some time. At this time the elders carefully address one another as *ma agii* ("my friend"), which shows, as Lugbara cynically remark, that they probably dislike each other in their hearts—"why else call a man your friend?" The visits are accompanied by gifts of beer, which become larger and larger on each occasion, to show one's good intentions and also to show up the other side's meanness. Finally negotiations start about the amount of bridewealth and the actual beasts concerned. The word for "to marry" is *je*, the word used for "buy," "exchange," or "barter." It should not be translated as "to buy" in this context, for the simple reason that this translation refers only to the modern economic activity of purchase with money, which was not traditional. But it may be translated as "exchange": the power of procreation and the sexual rights held in the woman by her father and her minimal lineage are transferred to her husband's lineage in return for certain property.

The marriage payments consist of certain objects. There is first a bull, the "bull of seduction." This bull is the same as that transferred for seduction of an unmarried girl. Lugbara say logically that a husband must in the nature of events seduce his wife unless someone else has done so already, and so this bull must be transferred. The transfer thus represents the sexual rights in the woman. In theory, if a bull has already been paid for her by a previous lover, it would not be transferred by the husband, but I know of no such case, as it would be regarded as insulting to the girl's family. There are then about seven head of cattle, which represent the procreative power of the woman. The "cattle" may in fact be goats, and today even money, bicycles, and other goods are known to be transferred instead, although this is unusual. If there is later a divorce, the cattle are returned, less one for every child born, the children remaining with the husband. The equivalence of cattle and children is here shown very clearly. Arrows are also transferred. They are a form of currency for use in certain situations, of which this is one. Several hundred arrows are collected from both the father's and mother's kin of the bridegroom, and handed over to the bride's father who in turn distributes them among her paternal and maternal kin. The transfer of arrows marks the establishment of the ties of affinity between the two lineages. Finally there are gifts of beer given to the girl's mother, to recompense her for the loss of her daughter, to heal her grief, and also to enable her to get a

---

[1] Young men say that they like to "test" a girl to see whether she is likely to make a good wife. If she succumbs to their blandishments she is likely to prove promiscuous and therefore a bad wife, but if she does not, the boys may not wish to visit her. It seems rather unfair on the girl.

substitute for a few days to help in the home. The beer represents, partly at any rate, the role of the girl as a domestic worker in her mother's home.

There may be a period of several weeks or even months between the agreement in the negotiations and the actual marriage. This period has as its main elements the symbolic death of the bride, and her capture by the groom's lineage. The girl covers herself with chalk and ashes, and wails, while her mother and sisters do the same and may sing songs and dance a special women's mourning dance. She is taken from her homestead by her husband and his lineage "brothers," with mock fighting against her brothers; this sometimes becomes serious, as there is always tension between affinally linked lineages. They are ready to quarrel over the bridewealth and the treatment of the wife at her new home, and there is also resentment at losing a daughter. Her mother is consoled by presents of cloth, beer, and money. It is said that traditionally this took all day, but today it is usually over within an hour or two, and the practice is not always observed. The girl then goes to her new home where she and her husband spend several nights and days in a hut alone. There are no public tests for virginity, although the husband's mother is said usually to make sure that the girl is in fact a virgin; but today many Lugbara admit that by no means all girls are virgins at marriage, and to have public tests and declarations would merely be embarrassing to everyone. Nonetheless, it is a topic of conversation and interest and is sure to be brought up if there are quarrels later.

A newly married wife "fears" or respects her husband, his father, mother, and brothers. She sits quietly on the ground when they are present and waits for them to speak before speaking to them herself. She puts a mat and a stool down for them when they enter the homestead, and cooks food for them, since "it is their homestead, here." She may not eat with them (although a man with only one wife usually eats with her when they have no visitors and are alone in their hut). A wife of long standing is on easier terms with her husband and may eat with him alone without fearing displeasure from his kin. At first she is shy before her husband's brothers because one of them may later inherit her, and they refer to and address her as "our wife."

When the bride becomes pregnant the marriage becomes more settled, and when she is a mother of a son it is complete. If she does not become pregnant it is said that the blessing which her father gave her on her marriage day, by spitting on her forehead, was not given with a good heart, and visits are made to persuade him to bless her properly. If she does not conceive within six months or so there is usually quarreling and the wife is sent home and the bridewealth demanded back, or a sister may be sent in her place. Although her own lineage will try to blame the matter on the husband's lineage, usually by accusing them of witchcraft, it is generally accepted that barrenness of the wife is the cause. Barrenness and adultery by a wife are grounds for divorce, although adultery is usually first punished by beating. Wives are expected to visit their natal homes regularly, taking gifts and returning with them, and the brothers-in-law are also expected to visit and to behave as friends. A good wife loves her husband, looks after his needs, and brings him girls to sleep with who may later become wives. A good husband loves his wife, does not beat her too much, and treats her exactly equally in every respect with her co-wives. In a polygynous household there is invariably tension between the co-wives, although a senior wife with a strong personality can keep her juniors in check; but the slightest favoritism by the husband will release hostility and quarreling about his head— and the fact that there is a word for "favorite wife" (the young and pretty one who is favored sexually if not in other ways), which is used as a term of abuse, shows that tension is expected. Co-wives are also said to ensorcell one another, and especially one another's children. However, Lugbara wives appear to the observer to be very free. They visit their kin frequently; they may stay away for long periods and are then suspected of adultery, but husbands can do little about it; if they are beaten or mistreated they run away to their brothers who may themselves come immediately to beat the husband—it is common for wives who run away to wait until they have a newborn child, and then run home with it so that the baby is a hostage to ensure conciliatory behavior by the husband. About two marriages in ten end in divorce, the usual reasons being adultery and barrenness on the part of the wives. In a polygynous society of this kind the husband cannot himself commit adultery merely by sleeping with other girls, provided they are themselves unmarried.

However, divorce occurs less frequently after the birth of children than before, especially of male children. When a wife has had a child who has survived the first few years of life,[2] her husband's lineage transfer a beast to her father's lineage, and this marks the acceptance of the wife by the husband's lineage as a mother of their children. After that her position in the household is eased greatly. She need no longer observe the formal rules of avoidance in private (although she will continue to do so in public) and her mother-in-law will cease to see her as a rival for her son's affection and will accept her as an ally, as a fellow-wife living in a strange lineage home.

If a woman is divorced, she returns to the care of her natal lineage. She is in a difficult position. Divorced women are usually regarded as flighty and difficult to control. They lead lives free of many of the irksome duties of a wife, and although they are often almost disowned by their own lineage if they do not remarry quickly, many women today prefer this status to that of a wife subject to domestic discipline and having to respect her affines. Nonetheless, these women are few and have a generally low status. Lugbara values decree that a woman should be married and have children—it is said that "the work of women is to bear children"—and only those women who are barren become permanently divorced. They often acquire position of a different order by becoming traders or pot makers, or, if they are able to, become diviners.

A woman who is past the menopause becomes a "big woman." She is in some contexts regarded as socially a man, and may take part in ritual,

---

[2] At the time of my stay, one child in three died during the first year of life.

share her husband's portion of sacrificial meat, and even take his position in some lesser rites if he is absent. She may represent him at oracle seances and can offer certain sacrifices, and when he dies she may "guard" his shrines. The curse of such an old woman is greatly feared and she may exercise considerable authority over her children and other kin.

A widow is inherited by one of her husband's successors in the lineage, usually either a brother or a son by another wife. After the period of mourning, she lives alone in her hut and is visited at night by as many of the possible inheritors as may wish to do so. When she decides to stay with a particular one, she hands him a hoe one morning as a sign of her approval of him as her pro-husband. Lugbara say that the "minds of widows are strong" and that they enjoy their power of choice. The new union is not a new marriage but a continuation of the old one. Children born to a widow after inheritance regard the pro-husband as their social and legal father—this is the institution of widow inheritance and not the true levirate.[3]

An old widow may refuse to be inherited and choose to be protected by one of her own sons, who builds her a hut where she ekes out a rather pathetic existence until she dies. However, a man regards his mother with great respect, and although old and poor she may hold considerable status and be treated with overt respect by those around her.

Kin by Marriage

It is clear that for the Lugbara marriage is not merely a union between two individuals but one between two lineages and two clusters of kinsfolk. By the rule of exogamy, these lineages must be unrelated, or only distantly related (people of the same clan do in fact marry if the tie is a remote one). Throughout a marriage the ties of a woman to her natal kin are remembered and are important. The observer is soon aware of the sense of responsibility people have for their sisters and daughters married elsewhere, and regular visits are made to see that they are well.

A marriage creates new ties of kinship between the two groups. The first is that of affinity, marked by the transfer of arrows, as I have mentioned. The second, which is made by the birth of a child, is that of maternal kinship between the child and his mother's lineage. The tie of affinity is centered on the relationship between the brothers-in-law (*otu*), who should regard one another as equals and friends. But they are usually, at first at any rate, suspicious of each other; the wife's brother may resent having lost a sister, and her husband often

---

[3] Neither do the Lugbara practice ghost-marriage or woman-marriage, institutions frequently found in association with the levirate (Evans-Pritchard 1951). When I told Lugbara of these Nuer practices they were amazed and scornful, asking: "What kind of fools are these? When a man dies, he dies, his body rots. . . . We are as we are here, we are not like those people in the Sudan, indeed."

resents having given what he considers too much bridewealth. Much depends on the wife's behavior and the husband's treatment of her: if she soon bears children and is a good wife, and if he treats her well, the brothers-in-law usually do respect and like each other. But I have known many brothers-in-law who regarded each other as virtual enemies and who waited for opportunities to score against one another and to shout abuse and brawl.

When a child is born the tie of maternal kinship is created between the child and his maternal kin. This, unlike that of affinity, is a tie of "blood," and a very intimate and important one for Lugbara. A man regards his sister's child "like his own child. Are they not of one blood? Is not his mother my own sister?" The sister's child knows that he can expect affection and help from the mother's brother throughout his life. As I have said earlier, a man will turn to his mother's brother for land or assistance if he should quarrel with his own family. The mother's brother will always assist him, thus enabling him to score against his sister's son's father, who is his own brother-in-law.

At the basis of the relationship between brothers-in-law and that of a man and his sister's son is a resentment at having lost a sister to another lineage. Lugbara stress this, saying that if only the sister had been born a man she would have begotten children for her own lineage, but because the Creator Spirit made her a woman, she has to bear children for another group. Her children are none-theless very close to her own kin, who protect them; this is continued after their death, when the sister's son sets special shrines for his mother's brother's ghost.

The ambivalence in the relationship between mother's brother and sister's son is typical, of course, in patrilineal societies. In Lugbara it is expressed formally in two ways. One is that the kinship term used is a reciprocal one, *adro;* although of different generation, they are formally made equal in status by each using the same term of address toward the other. The other is by use of "joking" between a man and his mother's brother, but even more between him and his mother's brother's wife. She is called *o'da,* which is both a kin term and also the verb "to joke." "Joking" takes the form of obscene insults between them when they meet, most references in the insults being sexual. The "joking" is obligatory, and it is thought that a man who does not joke will later get scabies as a punishment for ignoring correct kinship behavior. Lugbara say that a man insults his mother's brother's wife because if he (the sister's son) had been born a member of his mother's lineage he might later have inherited that particular woman when she became a widow. A man may—and should—take food and other things from his mother's brother's compound ("It should have been his food, but his mother was born a woman and not a man"), and the mother's brother's wife is a form of property also: he cannot take her as he does food, but insults her instead. Lugbara say, "You respect your mother's brother's wife but you treat her like a 'thing' also." To insult her is a way of making the distinction between the two lineages, for to use "joking" insults to a member of one's own lineage would lead to immediate fighting and probable mystical punishment.

The ties between individual kin through women are recognized also between their lineages. The collective forms of the kinship terms are used to apply to them: *adropi* (mother's brother's people) and *otupi* (wife's brother's people). They can refer to one's mother's family cluster, to her minor or major lineage, and even to her subclan. *Adropi* is used to refer to the distant groups that are known to be in some way related by maternal kinship which I have mentioned in Chapter 3. In theory there is a joking relationship recognized with such groups also, but the "joking" is mild. Any obscenity of the kind used with the true mother's brother and his wife is thought out of place and is usually resented.

6

Spirit and the Ancestors

Offenses and Sins

I HAVE MENTIONED that when people are related by close kinship the principal sanctions for proper behavior between them are religious. By this I mean that the Lugbara believe these sanctions are brought into operation by the Creator Spirit, ancestors and their ghosts, or various kinds of spirit; with these agents may be included witches and sorcerers, for although they are thought to be ordinary living men and women their powers are believed to come from Spirit and to be of a different order from the skills and abilities of normal people. In the next two chapters I shall discuss certain aspects of Lugbara religion from this point of view, to show how religious beliefs and practices act as means of controlling social behavior.

The lineage is the basic Lugbara social group, inasmuch as almost all social relations are conceived in lineage terms. For Lugbara the dead are as much members of the lineage as the living, and as its senior members they are respected and their wishes obeyed. Respect is the basis of ideal behavior toward both living and dead senior men, and provided that juniors respect seniors and women respect men, Lugbara consider that the well-being of the lineage and community is assured. It is only when men cease to respect their seniors that things go wrong and the various social sanctions I have mentioned have to be brought into play.

We may distinguish hostility between groups that is expressed in feud and warfare and that expressed by other means. Violence is the antithesis of correct behavior between close kin. A group of kin should not resolve its disputes by such means, especially when it is a small group with a single elder who has authority within it. I have said that where mutually recognized authority, sanctioned by appeal to common ghosts, breaks down, self-help is used in its place. The converse is that the resort to self-help destroys the recognition of common authority and representation. When two closely related lineages resort

61

to violence it is a sign that their formerly recognized common authority no longer exists.

Disputes about trespass, assault, disobedience of elders' authority, and so on, occur at all levels of the lineage, although they may be settled differently. The minimal lineage recognizes the internal domestic authority of the elder; wider segments do not. But the major lineage has other means which minimize the risk of overt hostility. One is that it is exogamous: it may not be the widest exogamous segment of the subclan, but the prohibition of intermarriage within it is rigidly maintained, whereas that beyond may occasionally be broken and the group split into two. This does not occur frequently, but any subclan has a few cases within the last generation or two. Within this lineage, however, sexual relations (as apart from marriage) are regarded as true incest; beyond it Lugbara accept them as taking place but unless followed by pregnancy or too flagrantly obvious it is unlikely that either the living or the dead will take much notice. But incest within the lineage is thought to be followed by mystical sanctions sent by the dead and by Spirit. Adultery within this segment is also sinful, being a breach of close fraternal relations (unless performed at the request of an impotent or absent husband). Beyond it adultery is followed by fighting or compensation. It is also the group within which homicide is fratricide, for which there is no humanly awarded punishment. Assault, especially if against an older man, is also more of a sin within this range than if beyond it; the latter leads to counterassault, the former to mystical sanctions being brought into play. All these offenses within this segment are in the nature of sins, their sinfulness lying in their being expressions of the rejection of true values of patrilineal kinship. At this range sanctions for orderly conduct are mystical, to do with the ghosts and ancestors. Accusations of witchcraft also occur as substitutes or replacements for overt violence. Relations with more distantly related lineages are sanctioned by the feud. This is also the range to which personal terms of kinship are used.

Most offenses within the lineage, especially incest and fratricide, are called by the term *ezata*. *Eza* is to "destroy" or "spoil," and *ezata* is "destruction" or "destroying"; it was given to me once as "the deed that destroys good words," and a Christian pastor translated it for me as "sin." It is said of a man who commits incest, adultery, or who persistently assaults and disobeys his close agnates that he is "a man with sin." It is contrasted with *yeta onzi* ("bad deeds"), which need not be concerned with lineage values. But it is not so much the intrinsic nature of the offense as the degree of closeness between offender and victim that is significant. Sins are mystically punished, by the dead and by Spirit. "Bad deeds" are rewarded by human response, although the dead and Spirit may also enter into the affair.

There are several other categories of relationship for which there are recognized sanctions. The individual relations between people who are kin but of different lineages are sanctioned by various curses, of which the most feared is that by a man's mother or grandmother (who are, of course, not of his lineage). There are also sicknesses brought by maternal ghosts for breaches of proper behavior by a man to his mother's brother's people. There are the relations between neighbors, controlled by fear of ostracism and witchcraft and sorcery. All the offenses concerned with these relationships are "bad deeds," rather than sins.

Spirit and the Nature of Man

Before discussing the cult of the dead, something should be said about the nature of man and Spirit.[1] Lugbara regard Spirit as an all-pervasive power that stands outside men and beyond their control. It is omnipotent and timeless, and can create and destroy men and send them various sicknesses, disasters, and punishments as well as good and prosperity. Spirit is both good and evil. Spirit as a creator is known as *Adroa 'ba o'bapiri* (Spirit the creator of men), *Adroa onyiru* (good Spirit) or *Adroa 'bua* (Spirit in the sky). Spirit is invisible and "in the wind," and is not personalized, because Spirit created persons and it can hardly therefore be a person itself. Linguistically the form *Adroa* or *Adronga* is the diminutive, since it is thought to be remote from men and not come into direct contact with them.

Besides the transcendent aspect of Spirit in the sky, there is also the immanent form on the surface of the world. This is known as *Adro,* the diminutive form of which is *Adroa.* This aspect of Spirit is thought to have the form of a tall man, white in color, cut in half down the middle, and hopping about on its one leg. It lives in streams, bushland, and on mountains, and if seen will kill and eat the person who glimpses it. It is often known as *Adro onzi* (evil Spirit), and is greatly feared.[2] This aspect of Spirit comes into direct contact with men, and can harm them in many ways. *Adro* also possesses girls and gives them the power of divination. *Adro* is said to have children, *adroanzi* ("*Adro*-children"), who are spirits of various kinds that live in streams, hills, and trees; they also guard rain groves. They have the form of small men and women, and can become visible, but a man who sees them dies. *Adroa, Adro,* and the *adroanzi* are found throughout Lugbara. In addition, each clan has its own *adro*-spirit, a manifestation of the power of Spirit that was concerned in the original genesis of each clan. Clans are linked together in this way, as well as having their separate ancestors. There are no rites associated with Spirit, except for certain prayers made to it at times of famine or disaster. Spirit comes into contact with men by sending sicknesses and disasters, and for men to contact it they must use diviners, prophets, or other persons who can communicate with it and who can interpret its various manifestations in the form of sickness, lightning, and epidemics.

When people die, they cease to be "people of the world outside" and become "people who have died" or "people in the earth." They are still "people" or "persons" (*'ba*), that is, human beings with social and moral re-

---

[1] In Middleton 1960*b* I used the term God for what I now prefer to call Spirit.

[2] One of the older-fashioned terms for a European is *Adro,* because Europeans are white and are believed to eat the people they take to hospitals and prisons.

sponsibility, as contrasted to "things" (*afa*) such as clients, babies, and young women, none of whom possesses social responsibility. The dead are said to live somewhere beneath the surface of the world, but people do not know exactly what their life is like. The belief in an afterlife is shadowy and unimportant, and there are no beliefs in heaven or hell or any rewards after death for offenses or good deeds while alive. "Our ancestors" are benevolent and wish well for their descendants, whom they protect and guide, but punish for sins. Although a dead person's character and personality are remembered for a few years, he is not regarded as malevolent after death even if so regarded while alive. Ancestors are thought to be aware of what goes on among their living kin, and discuss them among themselves. It is said that they like to say: "Now our child gives us food, and we are glad." To give food is a sign of close kinship.

A living man has certain elements. He has first a body, which becomes a corpse when dead and rots away in a few years; it is unimportant and "goes nowhere" after death. When alive a body contains breath, which at death goes no one knows where. Breath is a sign of life but has no great importance in itself. More important are certain invisible and spiritual elements: the *orindi*, the *adro*, and the *tali*. Of these the most important is the *orindi*, which I translate as "soul." The soul is said to be in the heart, and is the element that makes a man act responsibly as a social being and member of a lineage. At death it leaves the body and goes to Spirit in the sky; later it is contacted by a diviner and returns to earth where it lives at a shrine set for it. It is aware of what goes on among the living, and can in some mystical manner communicate with certain of the living and can send sickness to living sinners. When back in the shrine it becomes known as *ori*, which I translate as "ghost." Any dead person, man, woman, or child, becomes an ancestor (*a'bi*), but only certain of these become ghosts. "Ancestors" are all a man's dead kinsfolk, and although no man can relate the names of all his ancestors he nonetheless knows that they have lived and that after death they are somewhere in the earth beneath him. But only those whose souls have been given shrines are ghosts. A child rarely becomes a ghost, because his soul is small, and the same applies to most women. It is men who leave sons behind to place shrines for them who become ghosts. In effect, of course, this means that only those ancestors who are remembered in genealogies are also ghosts. An ancestor who becomes a ghost does not thereby cease being an ancestor, but is rather an ancestor who in death is known to be responsible toward his dead kin; and this is expressed by his being given a shrine at which sacrifices are made to him.

After death the soul of a man may be seen by his living kin as a specter (*atri*), which is an omen that he has died unhappily and that reparation of some kind must be made to him. Usually contact is made by a diviner, and the wishes of the dead man satisfied. He then rests content and a shrine is later made to his name. It is sometimes also said that the shadow is a form of the soul, but this belief is unimportant, except that witches can harm a victim by treading on his shadow.

The other elements are the *adro* and *tali*. I need not discuss them at length here. *Adro* is put into the body at birth, or conception (it is not known which) by Spirit. It is a sign of man's divine creation, and can be translated as "spirit." After death it leaves the body and goes off into the bushland, where it becomes one of the *adroanzi* or spirits of the water, hills, or trees. The *tali* is the element that enables a man to have influence over those around him, and it increases in power during his lifetime. After death it leaves the body and lives in a shrine where all the *tali* of past members of the lineage are. *Tali* is a word used for any manifestation of the power of Spirit, such as a place where lightning has struck, or a mystical power such as rainmaking or divination.

Death and Burial

Death marks the beginning of an elaborate *rite de passage,* for both the dead person and for his living kin. The mortuary rites of Lugbara are the only rites or ceremonies that attract large numbers of people, and are highly important in Lugbara society. Almost every other rite is the concern of a small lineage and neighborhood only, but the mortuary rites of an important man may attract people from neighboring subtribes and last for days or even weeks: I have known cases in which they were not completed for over a year. At death a man's physical body is disposed of and forgotten, and those parts of him that do not become ancestor and ghost go to the domain of Spirit, either in the sky or in the bushland. Ancestors are important only to their living kin, in particular, members of their lineage; they have no significance to other people. A dead man has relations with both living and dead kin; Lugbara know little about the latter relations, but the former are modeled on those he had with the living while he was alive. At death the kinship status of the dead person remains, but other aspects of his social personality are extinguished.

The corpse is buried with certain objects that represent his status as a man, woman, or child, as such, and with certain objects associated with any status he may have acquired outside the lineage. With a man are buried his quiver, his favorite drinking gourd, and his elder's stool if he had been an elder. These objects symbolize the positions he had held during his lifetime: the quiver that of a young man who is a warrior and hunter, the drinking gourd that of the mature man who drinks and talks with his kin and neighbors, and the stool that of the elder. In addition, if he had become an oracle operator he is buried with his rubbing-stick and pots he used for the boiling-water oracle. With a woman are buried her beads (which represent her position as a girl), the three fire stones of her hearth ("the stones where she cooked food for her husband"), and the smaller of the two grinding stones with which she has ground flour; these last two represent her status as wife and mother in her husband's lineage. The grinding stone is that which she actually held while grinding, the one she chose herself from the rounded pieces of granite in the stream bed. The larger, lower grinding stone is not vested with her personality as is this upper stone, and passes to her daughter. Her pots, gourds, and other household utensils are broken by her brother, who also scatters the grain from her granary over the compound and pulls the thatch from her hut roof. This is done "because these are her own things, but are little": she made them but her personality is not in them as it is in the other objects. Both men and women are buried with beans, simsim, and heads of eleusine, the three traditional staple crops of the Lugbara, about which there are myths that tell of their being tilled by the heroes (other crops are later importations). The burial of these objects and foodstuffs is in no way in preparation for any kind of journey to the land of the dead. Lugbara state this quite explicitly and say they are put with the corpse "because he would have eaten them. Now who will eat them? Let us pour them over the corpse." For a woman, then, her brother (her closest kinsman) destroys her possessions. The objects buried with her symbolize her status as a wife, and after death it is her status as an ancestress that remains significant in her son's lineage, not that of a wife as such. She is buried in her husband's compound, not taken back to her natal home, if she dies where she is married.

The corpse of a child is buried with the little basket that was used to cover his head when being carried on his mother's back, and with a small gourd used to contain the simsim oil with which he was cleansed.

Other possessions are inherited. They are primarily the dead person's livestock, and the stones of the shrines that a man has set up himself. Both men and women may acquire their own livestock during their lives, by working or trading, and these are their individual property. Livestock are "things of the lineage" and in theory they may be used only for bridewealth or sacrifice, never merely killed for meat.

The grave as such is not important, and is soon forgotten. An adult man is buried inside his first wife's hut, in the center of the floor. The grave is from four to six feet deep, with a recess in the center of the floor in which the corpse is laid, with legs straight and right hand under the head. The head is placed in the direction of either Mount Liru or Mount Eti, according to whether the dead person is High or Low Lugbara. A papyrus sleeping mat is placed at the bottom of the grave, and then the hide of one of the dead man's bulls killed for the purpose by his brothers. Today the corpse is also usually wrapped in white cloth. This and the washing of the corpse is done by his lineage sisters, chosen from the major lineage and of the same generation as the dead man. The grave is dug and the corpse buried by "mother's brothers," "because he was our son, there." Over the corpse in its recess are placed granite slabs to prevent earth from falling onto it. The grave is then filled in with earth and a cairn of stones raised on top of it; after a few years this is moved and the site cultivated. Women are buried in their huts likewise, except that they lie on their left side and no cattleskin is placed beneath the body. Children are buried in the same way, either in the mother's hut or in the hut doorway.[3] A miscarriage of a fetus of over three months counts as the death of a child, and mourning and burial are as for those of a child.

Elders and very senior women (those who are the senior sisters of

---

[3] Father Ramponi states that twins are buried in double-mouthed pots, but I have been unable to confirm this (see E. Ramponi, 1937).

men who become elders, and so who would have themselves been elders had they not been born women) are buried outside the huts, in the compound, usually near the chief wife's granary, under which are the ghost shrines. The burial is the same as for other people, but a thatched roof three or four feet high is often built over the grave and a barkcloth tree planted at its head. They are buried outside "because they are big" and thus feared. If buried inside the huts the widows' bodies will become "bad." Wailing for an elder begins when his cattle low after his death. A rainmaker is also buried in the compound, but whereas an ordinary person is buried to wailing and dancing, a rainmaker is buried in silence, at night, lest he turn into a leopard at the burial. This is also occasionally done for an old and highly respected elder. Dead lepers are exposed in the bushland, without burial rites being performed for them. They are believed to have acquired the disease by being cursed by their kin or by committing incest, and are therefore said to be beyond the ties of kinship. The same applies to persons killed by lightning or epidemics, both of which are regarded as actions of Spirit.

The burial is mainly the affair of the immediate lineage kin, especially those of the same generation, and of mother's brothers only. Other kin enter the compound to watch and wail, and they also wail and dance outside the compound; I describe the dancing below.

The dead person's mother, mother's sisters, and widows do not touch the corpse. They wail loudly and cover their heads and bodies with dust and earth, and they may throw themselves on the ground and roll about in the ashes of the fire of the compound, which is put out when the death occurs. The mother and the widows do not remove the dust and ashes, nor shave their heads or wash until the end of the period of mourning. Both mourning and the ashes used are called *uri* ("fear" or "respect"). These women have special cries of mourning, which are different from those used by the lineage sisters, which are in their turn different from those used by other kin and by neighbors.

Mourning affects only the immediate kin of the dead person, and especially the widow or widower, who enters into seclusion until the end of the mourning period. During this time they live in a small hut built for the purpose, and may neither wash nor shave their heads, which must remain whitened with finely powdered ashes. Other members of the immediate family, and sisters' children, are not secluded but do not shave their heads for the same period. They wear ashes on their faces for four days if the dead person was a man, or three if a woman.

The lineage sisters who touch the corpse are regarded as ritually unclean. After the burial they wash in the nearest stream before they mix with other people, and they are not allowed to oil their bodies (a sign that the pollution has not finally been removed). The mother's brothers who prepare the grave are not so polluted. They merely wash and rejoin the dancers afterward. This washing is different from that of the lineage sisters, who go formally to the stream together, often under the direction of a diviner, but the mother's brothers regard their lustration as something rather everyday.

All other kin who attend the burial shave their heads, especially those who actually enter the compound. Lugbara say this is done to be "clean," and thus not be harmed by the corpse. They may also put ashes on their heads, but usually only on their foreheads and not over the entire face. Women, however, do not wear fresh leaves as apparel, but wear those of the day before. The compound is not swept, and is left dirty until after the end of the period of mourning.

Once the corpse is buried there starts the process of changing the dead person's status from that of a living to a dead kinsman. As a dead kinsman he is both respected and feared, in much the same way as a living man when he becomes senior in lineage and family position. On the whole the dead are regarded as beneficent, the origins of law and order and custom. Their ability to send sickness to their living descendants is part of their role as the guardians of morality, and it is accepted that they do not do so wantonly or without adequate reason. But they are also feared. This is true especially of the newly dead, since it is not known what grudges they may hold toward their living kin at the time they die. A man who knows he is about to die calls for his close lineage kin to him and speaks his last words, in which he is said to designate his lineage successor and to bring into the open any grudges that he may hold. In fact, the living tend to interpret the last words of a dying man as they themselves feel best for the lineage. Immediately after death the soul goes to the place of Spirit in the sky, outside the control of living men, and it is at this time that any resentment toward them by the living may be expressed openly, and they may haunt the living as specters to show that they have died with grudges. Once the dead become full ancestors and ghosts, any resentment toward them is ideally not permitted, since by then it should have been dispersed by the diviner contacting the soul. The ambivalent attitude toward a senior kinsman is largely an aspect of the relationship to him as a known individual, which lessens after his death as the memory of him fades.

Resentment may, however, be expressed overtly at his burial. The death of an important man is followed by a period when many of the obligations of kinship are temporarily in abeyance. This period is marked by permitted license in behavior between kin, and by such things as the non-sweeping of the lineage compounds.

At the burial the dead man's successor and other men of the minimal lineage concerned speak of him and recount the "words of the ancestors." They bring certain sacred leaves, which are associated with Spirit, dip them in water, and place them on the ground. If that evening a jackal or other night creature defecates on them they know that the dead man has died with a "bad" heart, but if there is no excrement on the leaves the next morning it is a sign that he died content and by the will of Spirit, about which he cannot complain. This is done for all men who leave children, and for old women, but not for young women and children. Before the grave is closed the lineage kin stand around it, address the dead man, and express any overt resentment toward him. One such address that I heard included the words:

Now you are dead. You fear now. . . . It is good that you fear. . . . You have begotten children and done many things. . . . Now you are dead, like

a pot that is broken. If your heart is bad, then tomorrow we shall see. . . .
Now you are dead and your words are little. . . .

At the burial also a bull or goat must be given to the deceased's own
true mother's brother. This is the "corpse beast." If the deceased is a woman,
her agnates are given a beast as well, known also as "corpse beast." The burial
does not take place until this is done, for until they have accepted it, the mother's brother and, if a woman, her lineage kin, are not satisfied as to the cause
of death. If they are not satisfied, they usually suspect witchcraft. The dead
man would then return to haunt his lineage, or a woman to haunt her husband's lineage.

Death Dances

So far I have mentioned some of the events that are connected with the
change of a person's status from a living to a dead member of the lineage. But
he is at the center of a network of ties between lineages and groups of kin. At
his death there is a rearrangement of these ties. These realignments are of
relationships between the minimal lineage and other groups and are made at
death dances.

The dances start after the death, usually immediately after the burial.
There are two sets of dances, the *ongo* and the *abi*. *Ongo* is the generic term
for "dance," and these dances are highly elaborated. There are many variations
but always two main dances: the "wailing dance" and the "leaping dance."
Each consists of several distinct dances with their own songs telling of the dead
man's life and way of dying. As in most Lugbara songs, there is much bitter
and sarcastic allusion to the failings of other lineages, and so there is a good
deal of airing of grievances and thereby disposing of them.[4]

Both men and women dance, although the main dances in the center of
the arena—usually a cleared space outside the compound—are done mostly by
men only, the women being on the periphery. Much beer is drunk, and because men carry spears and arrows there is often fighting. Women carry wands,
and senior women, those who are the first born of sets of brothers and sisters and
therefore "like men," may carry quivers. In the dances men stand by generation,
not by lineage or family. The team consists of the men of a lineage. Lineages
which enter the arena first thereby show their seniority over other lineages, and
fighting often occurs as they jostle to take their position as a previous dance
ends. There may also be brawling among the dancers themselves: those of the
same generation dance side by side, leaping up and down, and to jolt one's
neighbor can lead to argument and fighting. These dances are not solemn occasions. Because dances may continue for days and nights at a stretch, with the
drums never stopping,[5] many people are soon in a trancelike condition and

---

[4] Lugbara themselves say that when a grievance is openly expressed anyone who
later takes it up will become ashamed and lose face.

[5] There are usually three drums; the "child," the "wife," and the "grandmother,"
and players change over from time to time without stopping the beat.

normally expected behavior may be relaxed. Lugbara recognize this, saying: "Death has destroyed the words, a big man is dead and we are like children with no one to help us." This behavior is expressed in many ways: by the fluidity of lineage relationships as seen in the jostling for seniority and the fighting; by the normally forbidden seduction of clan-sisters by young men, an accepted piece of bravado that is said "to show young men who are their clan-sisters" (the implication being that with lineage ties in temporary disarray people forget their relationships); and sometimes in the reversal of sexual roles, usually by young men wearing women's leaves as apparel, women leading men's dance teams, and so forth.

While the dancing is going on, couples run out of the throng of watchers to the outskirts of the arena. There the man cries his *cere* call[6] and shoots arrows into the bush (or mimics doing so) and the woman calls her *cere*. There is no expected relationship between the pair, except that they are never husband and wife; they may be lineage or other kin, or merely close friends. The expressed purpose of this action is that it "shows" other lineages that the pair wish to avenge the death. It is done only for adult men.

The observer soon sees that death dances are of great importance. They are the occasions for the greatest coming together of kinsfolk. There is little ceremonial or ritual at birth and marriage, and no initiation ritual. Large dances are said to have been held in the past at the first harvests in the year, but they were smaller than big death dances. Other dances, *koro* and *walangaa* ("dances of play"), are recent introductions, and the traditional *nyambi* dance of women, danced at a bride's leaving her natal home, attract only a small audience. But death dances are the cause for excitement and interest over a wide area, and the continual drumming and singing are audible for miles.

The *ongo* dances are performed immediately after the death; those for an important man may last for a week, those for a young man, a woman, or a child for only a day or so and be attended by only a few close kin. At various periods afterward, usually during the following harvest season when plenty of food and beer are easily available, the dances known as *abi* are held. These occur at odd times as groups of kin visit, and may continue for up to a year, and even longer for very important men. The occasions and the atmosphere at them are very different. The *ongo* are performed by close kin of the same lineage, the maternal kin, and groups which have married women of the dead man's lineage. They come "to dance the death dance" and "to wail," and bring arrows which are given to the dead man's close lineage kin. It is said, "You always give where you get your wife," and these arrows are a continuation of the bridewealth payments made earlier. They are given to "help" the dead man's lineage; they may be accompanied by gifts of food, and the visitors are

---

[6] The *cere* is a long, high-pitched falsetto whooping cry. Every adult man and woman has his or her own (to which words are fitted). They are traditionally called for help and at dances, and today men call them when coming home drunkenly from beer parties, so that they may be recognized in the dark, and also to show that they are "big." It is a deep insult to cry another person's *cere* except at the one occasion when a man's heir cries the dead man's call immediately after his death.

formally given food and beer. The *abi* dances are performed by groups of visiting affines who come "to rejoice." They come from those lineages which have supplied women as wives to the lineage of the dead man, and are given arrows in their turn. The "rejoicing" is because by paying respect and receiving arrows they show that the tie of affinity has been reaffirmed after being weakened by the death of the person who was the link between the two lineages.

The death dances are, as I have said, the occasions for the recognition of the rearrangement of ties between kin after a death. The ties that are formally stressed are those which cut across lineage affiliation. Although groups come to dance as lineages, it is the kinship relationship of them as a category (lineage, maternal, or affinal kin) that is stressed and not their lineage identity as such. People say, "Here are our mother's brothers who come to dance," rather than use the name of the lineage. Within the teams of dancers men of the same generation should dance together, and generations should succeed each other.

Death dances should be times of peace and amity, but they are frequently occasions of fighting and quarreling, as lineages compete for recognition of their seniority. This lack of any firm or generally accepted genealogical seniority between related lineages, and of any superior authority to determine such seniority, runs through much of Lugbara ritual. It is a point of continual discussion and competition, and a great deal of the cult of the dead is concerned with this competition. Death, especially of an elder, is a time when the segmentation of his lineage is likely, the succession to eldership providing a precipitating cause. The realignment between lineage segments is decided inside the dying man's hut during his last words, and later at the dances when it is formally stressed that lineage differences should be forgotten and generation unity stressed. What happens is that the lineage alignment that has been accepted hitherto, and has been maintained by the dead elder's authority, may now no longer be accepted and lineages struggle to claim seniority over their fellow lineages at the time of uncertainty.

I return to this point later, because the competition for relative status at death dances is not an isolated phenomenon. It continues between deaths in the form of competition for ancestral favor in the rites of the ghost cult, and also, of course, in secular alliances in feuds and court cases. Death dances provide one opportunity for attempting to get public acceptance of relative status, since these dances are the occasion of such wide gatherings of kin. I have considered them, briefly, before discussing ritual proper; but they may be understood as providing a climax, as well as a beginning, to competition waged between heads of families and lineages during the lifetime of a senior man.

Contacting the Soul

There remains only to bring the soul of the dead person into a permanent relationship with the living, a relationship which is centered physically upon shrines erected for it. This is done by three acts: contacting the soul "in the sky," settling any grudges and anger it may have toward the living, and building the shrine for it. These may all be done at the same time, or spread out over several weeks or even months. Much depends on the dead person's status—the higher, the more likely is the process to be spread out—and on whether the living kin have the food and beer needed for these rites (it depends therefore to some extent on the time of year).

The soul, especially that of a senior man, is contacted either if sickness comes upon one of his kinsmen and an oracle states that it is sent by the recently dead soul, or if someone dreams about the dead person or sees him as a specter. Contact is made by a diviner, a woman who has the mystical power to speak with the dead soul. She discovers whether or not it has died contentedly or with grudges against the living. If the former, the diviner erects a shrine, but if the latter, the grudge must first be settled. Later the chief heir of the dead person erects a shrine to his ghost when he first makes a sacrifice to it.

Shrines are of many kinds. The principal shrines are those erected for a ghost of an ancestor. They are known in most of Lugbaraland as *orijo* ("ghost house") and consist of pieces of granite formed into a rough house or shelter and placed under the chief wife's granary; they may take the form of a miniature hut with a thatched roof. A ghost does not have merely a single shrine, but may have several, one in each of its patrilineal descendants' compounds. A ghost shrine is named after its incumbent. It is not thought to dwell in the shrine but rather to use it as a place where it may receive sacrificial food and beer from those of its descendants who live in that particular compound.

There are many types of shrines set for the dead. The ghost shrines are the most important, because it is the ghosts who most often send sickness. Shrines are also set for the ancestors as ancestors, that is, including those ancestors who did not become ghosts because they left no sons behind; for the ghosts of mothers' brothers; for women of the lineage; and for many kinds of spirits. There is not the space in this account to give details of them all (Middleton 1960*b*, Chap. II).

7

The Cult of the Dead

The Ritual Position of the Elder

CERTAIN OFFENSES, those which I call sins, are followed by mystical sanctions and by sacrifice to the ghosts. These sanctions are put into operation and controlled by living people, who have the power both to interpret the actions and motives of the dead and to intercede with them to withdraw the sanctions when the time is appropriate.

Lugbara recognize that a lineage segments, and that quarreling and disputes are signs of incipient segmentation. Yet ideally there should be peace within it. Kin quarrel but the ideal of kinship is peaceful cooperation for the common good. Men are ambitious and want power, but for a man to be accused of personal ambition is to label him a deviant from the ideal, a man who thinks more of his own position than that of the welfare of the members of the lineage. A lineage vests authority in its elder; anyone else who tries to exercise power within the group threatens the elder's authority and therefore the well-being of the lineage. Undelegated power and authority cannot both be exercised within the same unit by different people. The problem here, of course, is to permit different people to hold ambitions which may be mutually incompatible. The head of a family within the family cluster has the duty of pressing the claims of his own family's members against those of the other families. He is expected to do this and his dependants will complain if he does not. Yet from the viewpoint of the total family cluster he should not do this but should discuss matters in amity with his fellow heads of families, and the head of a family frequently finds himself in a position of conflict. The ideal of the elder's behavior is that he should be quiet, dignified, slow in decision, and ready to act in union with his "brothers," the elders of other minimal lineages. The unity of the lineage is the ideal. But not all elders and senior men observe the ideal; younger men do so still less, and indeed in the past would not have been admired as warriors if they had. There is the feeling that younger men are more disruptive, because they lack the social maturity and experience of elders. The expected behavior (but not perhaps the ideal) of younger men thus in fact fits the position in which they find themselves, that of heads of junior families, exhorted by their own dependants to gain benefits for these families but subject to the over-all unity of the lineage and the authority of its elder. A young man who shows "slowness" is pointed out in old men's discussions as a man of promise, but he may find himself despised by his equals. The expected behavior of men of different levels of seniority in the lineage thus differs: a "youth" looks out for himself among his fellow youths but should obey his seniors; a "big youth," who has married and started a family, should fight for the rights of his wives in land and other resources, but must also recognize his responsibilities to the wider group; the "men behind" are the heads of joint families, usually of equal generation to elders but debarred from eldership by the vagaries of birth and genealogy; and, finally, the elders exercise authority for the good of all and must forget their simultaneous position as heads of their own families, which are only units of the lineages of which they are the heads. These levels of seniority are not formal, and there is no initiation into any of them.

In a similar way the relations between minimal lineages and the family clusters formed around them, and therefore between their elders, should be both of competition to maintain their separate rights and of unity and alliance in which mutual interests are paramount. An elder once said to me: "Elders often quarrel among themselves like young men; we are men and all men have bad hearts. But the ancestors do not quarrel among themselves." Although it is often said that the dead do in fact quarrel, in this context the meaning is clear. The "elder" who really joins under his own authority two related lineages is an ancestor.

Lugbara thus recognize fairly explicitly that divisive phases in the history of a lineage correspond to, and are expressed in, quarrelsomeness and ambition on the part of heads of segments, whereas cohesive phases correspond to "slowness" and wisdom in heads of segments. Both young, old, and dead members play these roles.

The elder's authority is sustained by certain sanctions, of which by far the most important are the ritual sanctions that are part of the cult of the dead. He has no physical force at his disposal. Above the level of the elder there is no superior authority except for the sporadic and occasional exercise of their powers by rainmakers and "men whose names are known." Traditional groups fought, or today have recourse to chiefs' courts, but both fighting and taking to court are opposed to the norms of kinship and close neighborhood. The only other sanctions, except for those of public opinion and the process of witchcraft, are those considered by Lugbara to be operated by the dead. The dead are supposed to bring sickness to their living kin as a response to an infringement of proper kinship behavior. They do so either at the invocation of living kin or on their own responsibility. Oracles are consulted to discover the agents concerned and the reasons for their sending sickness. The sickness is lifted by the promise of sacrifice, which is performed after the recovery of the sick person. Part of the rite of sacrifice is the communion of living and dead kin, and by it proper relations are restored. This is the process as Lugbara conceive it. The social reality is somewhat different. Much anthropological theory has tried to show that ritual is cohesive, that its performance maintains and strengthens a sense of interdependence and solidarity among people who perform the rites together as members of a congregation. This is true of Lugbara ritual. But it is only half the story. It provides a set of sanctions for the unity of the family cluster and its component segments. Communion at sacrifices makes for lineage cohesion. But at the same time competition between segments and lineages is played out in ritual terms. Living men compete among themselves for headship and authority, which are seen by the Lugbara largely in terms of the ability to invoke the dead against others. In a state society, men may compete to gain the approval of a king or chiefs. Lugbara, without kings or chiefs, see men's responsibilities for their actions toward kin and neighbors as being to the dead rather than toward other living persons. This was so traditionally and is so today. Chiefs exist (and with far greater powers than those held by anyone in the traditional system) but their authority is irrelevant as regards behavior of almost any kind between close kin.[1]

Ghost Invocation and Vengeance

The main aspect of the relationship between the dead and their living kin is that the dead send sickness to those living kin whom they consider to have harmed the well-being of the lineage. It is mainly the ghosts of the recently dead who are thought to do this: they are aware of the tensions and dissensions within the lineage, and know the personalities of the living. It is said that just as a father disciplines his son and expects respect from him, a man expects his dead father and father's brothers to take an interest in him, whereas more distant ghosts are not so concerned. It is said that the recently dead ghosts report the ill deeds of the living to the more distant ghosts, who deliberate on the matter and then decide whether or not to send sickness to punish the living evildoer; they then give instructions to the recently dead who send the actual sickness.

The relationship between dead and living members of the lineage is expressed most fully in the ritual of sacrifice. In many societies sacrifice is made to ancestors or gods periodically: at birth, harvests, or other recurrent occasions. Lugbara do not sacrifice on such occasions, but do so only as part of a process of events which starts with a person being sick. They believe that sickness is sent by the dead to "show" the living that they are displeased by their sinful behavior. The ritual guardian of the sick person (his father, or eldest brother, or if a wife, her husband) consults oracles to discover the identity of the ghost concerned and the nature of the sacrifice that will later be made to him. The sacrificial object for ghosts is an animal (for certain spirits and non-ghostly ancestors it may be grain or beer only). It is promised as sacrifice if the sick person recovers. After his recovery, the animal is sacrificed at the shrines, the meat is shared among the members of the lineage who gather together as a congregation, the patient is anointed and blessed and the matter is regarded as closed. If he does not recover, it is thought that the oracles were mistaken in their verdict, and they are either consulted again or it is thought that Spirit is involved and no offering is made. To sacrifice to Spirit would be presumptuous and pointless.

From the observer's viewpoint this process begins with a person being sick, in particular with the sickness known as *oyizu* ("growing thin"), a non-specific sickness or general malaise. But Lugbara see it differently. For them the process begins with the commission of sin, which is followed by either ghost invocation or ghostly vengeance. These phrases are my translations of the Lugbara expressions *ole ro* and *ori ka*. Literally *ole ro* means "to bring sickness (because of) indignation:" *ro* means to invoke the dead to bring sickness; *ole* means indignation, envy, or annoyance at sinful behavior. The invocation of the ghosts is done by a living person, typically an elder; but anyone whose father is dead may do so. He sits near his shrines in his compound and thinks about the sinner's behavior. His thoughts are known by the ghosts and they then send sickness to the offender. He "thinks these words in his heart"; he does not threaten or curse the offender. For a senior man to do this is part of his expected role. It is part of his "work," to "cleanse the lineage home." Indeed, an elder who does not do so when justified would be lacking in sense of duty toward his lineage. A man may invoke the dead to send sickness against any member of his family cluster and his minimal lineage, whether living in the family cluster's compounds or not. Within the family cluster are included lineage members, their wives, and attached kin such as sisters' sons. A man is thought not to invoke against sisters' sons living elsewhere: to discipline them is the duty of their own elders where they live. Lugbara often stress that elders are "like brothers," and may discuss the sins of their dependants among themselves. An offender will then be controlled by his own elder, even if another elder is the person who has been insulted or injured. The principle is that a senior man has the duty to maintain his authority over all members of his family cluster, whether or not they are members of his agnatic lineage. He has also authority, particularly in lineage matters though perhaps not in petty family matters, over all members of his lineage who live elsewhere. In theory, invocation may be by any man whose father is dead, even if he is a minor, and I know of cases of invocation by a child. But typically it is by a senior man, either an elder or the head of a family segment within the family cluster. Invocation may also be by a woman whose mother is dead; but this is rare.

A living man is thought to invoke the dead because he feels the sentiment of indignation over sin. The dead are also believed to be able to send sickness without invocation, on their own account. This is ghostly vengeance, *ori ka.* It is thought that the dead may think their dependents do not sacrifice to them often enough or do not remember them with respect, and they then send sickness to them.

Oracles

For the Lugbara, this whole process starts with the commission of a sin, followed by ghost invocation or ghostly vengeance, followed by sickness. Since ghost invocation and ghostly vengeance are mystical processes, it is necessary to have a means of discovering which of the ghosts are sending sickness, the reasons for their doing so, and the nature of the sacrifice they want made to them. For the outside observer, the process begins with sickness coming to a person, who has then to decide the reasons for it. In order to discover the "facts" behind the sickness, oracles are consulted, either by the sick person or, more usually, on his behalf by his ritual guardian. The ritual guardian is either his elder or the head of his family, and thus may in fact be the same person who has invoked the dead against him.

Oracles (*andri*) are said to have been given men by Spirit so that they could discover the "words" of the dead. They can tell whether sickness is sent to a person by the dead, by Spirit, by witches or sorcerers, or by spirits. Oracles know the identity of the dead responsible, but not of witches or sorcerers—to discover their identity a man must consult a diviner. There are several kinds of oracles, most of which are found throughout Lugbaraland. The most common, and the first always consulted, is the *acife,* or rubbing-stick oracle. This consists merely of a stalk of sorghum which is held in the operator's left hand and rubbed by a twist of grass or even by the fingers of the other hand. As it is rubbed the names of suspected agents of the sickness are put to it by the operator. When his fingers stick by their pressure the oracle is thought to have given that particular name. There are variants of the actual operation but they are all similar. Any man whose father is dead may operate his own rubbing-stick oracle, although a man will not do so for his own sickness; it is usual for an operator of another lineage to be consulted. It might seem that an operator can control the verdict of his oracle merely by the pressure of his fingers, and indeed this could be done. But it would hardly be necessary because it is irrelevant. The important point is that an oracle agrees with or denies only those names put before it. The names are chosen by the client, and the oracle selects one of them. The client does not put false names to the oracle, but only those of persons whom he thinks may have been offended by his behavior. Thus by definition the names are those of possible suspects and the oracle must select a person with a motive for invoking the dead. In addition to the names of people who may have been offended by sinful behavior, it is usual to put forward witchcraft as a suspect, without mentioning the identity of a possible witch. If the oracle selects witchcraft the client goes to a diviner to find the witch's identity. Thus an oracle cannot give a name which would be absurd because the sick person's own conscience selects the names to be put to it. In addition, the client gives background information about the people named to the operator, and there is no doubt that a good operator soon realizes who is the most likely suspect in his client's mind and may select that particular name.

Other oracles are more mechanical and are used to confirm the verdict of the rubbing-stick oracle. The chicken oracle is constructed of a round hole in the ground, on the edges of which marks are placed for names of suspects. The head of a chicken is cut off, the body fluttering around the hole and finally coming to rest against one of the marks. If three chickens come to rest against the same mark, the oracle confirms that particular name. The boiling-medicine oracle is constructed of a small fire in which are placed clay cups named for suspects. "Medicine" prepared by the operator is poured by him into the cups in turn, and that which boils over quickly confirms the name. The rat oracle is constructed merely of a rat-trap of stones. A name is put to it in the evening. If a male rat is caught, the name is confirmed; if a female or no rat is caught, the name is denied. There is also a pod oracle, in which seeds of a poisonous tree are heated and jump about on a piece of metal; the way they move and come to rest determines the verdict. There was formerly also a poison oracle in western Lugbara, taken from the Logo who use the Azande *benge* oracle, but this is now obsolete (Evans-Pritchard 1937).

The ritual guardian of the sick person thus finds out whether the agent sending the sickness is ghost, ancestor, or witch, whether the process has started with ghost invocation or ghostly vengeance, the reason for the sickness and the nature of the sin committed, and the kind of animal required for the sacrifice. In the case of sickness from the ghosts, he confirms the verdict of the rubbing-stick oracle. Typically, perhaps, the person who consults the oracles is himself the elder of the sick person and the man who has invoked the ghosts against him, but Lugbara see nothing odd in this situation, because they believe in the efficacy of the oracles and the honesty of the elder concerned.

The Rite of Sacrifice

The ritual of sacrifice consists of various elements: the consecration of the animal to be sacrificed; the ritual addresses; the killing and the offering of the animal; the blessing and anointing of the sick person; and the distribution of meat, blood, and beer among the living members of the lineage.

The animal is consecrated for a particular sacrifice. The ritual guardian takes the beast to the sick person's compound, after having kept certain taboos to be ritually pure. He places his left hand on the animal's back and says that if the patient recovers he will sacrifice the beast. It is led round the compound in a counterclockwise direction, four times if the patient is a man and three times if a woman. The beast is then stood at the compound entrance. If it urinates it is a sign that the patient will recover and the sacrifice will be made, but if it does not, or if the sky turns dark or it rains, it is a sign that Spirit "refuses," and that sacrifice to the ghosts is unnecessary; the oracles have lied or been mistaken, and Spirit has decided that the patient should not recover. Nothing can then be done except to wait for his death.

Sacrifice is made after the patient has recovered from the sickness. It is made at his compound, and he must be present. The ritual guardian supervises the ritual, although he may not perform every action himself. The members of the congregation, who are members of the minor or sometimes major lineage, assemble, after having kept certain taboos to acquire moral purity. At first they sit around the compound, members of each lineage sitting together as a group; they are given beer by the wives of the homestead, and chat and laugh together and discuss the matter at hand—whether the sacrificial animal is fat enough to provide them with good meat is usually the main item of conversation. There seems to the observer to be nothing particularly sacred about the occasion. It is only after the telling of the first ritual address that the nature of the meeting becomes more serious and reverent.

There are two formal ritual addresses. The first is said by the elder, who talks to both living and dead members of the lineage assembled there. He states merely that they have come to sacrifice on account of the recovery of the patient who has been "shown" his sins by the sickness. The address unites living and dead into a single congregation.

The sacrificial animal is then killed by having its throat cut by sisters' sons (who are not members of the lineage concerned). The blood is collected in a pot, the carcass scorched, skinned, and cut up, and the contents of the stomach and intestines squeezed out into another pot. The elder takes some of the blood, some small pieces of meat, and some porridge and places them in the ghost shrines. He also pours blood on the shrines. This is the central act of the rite: the ghosts are given food to eat and are thereby brought into communion with their living kin.

The second ritual address is then made, which is far more important than the first. The elder takes sacred leaves in his hand, leaves that are thought to represent fertility and that are liked by the dead because of their sweet smell and soft texture, and relates the details of the sin that has precipitated the sickness. Lugbara stress that when speaking a ritual address a man must speak the truth; if he lies, the effect of the rite is destroyed and it must be done again. The second address is usually long and involved, bringing in much semisecret lore of the lineage. It is often almost unintelligible without some knowledge of the history of the lineage and the personalities of its members. It includes much genealogical tradition, and its being made in a heightened ritual atmosphere makes genealogy and history into a single coherent body of lineage tradition and experience. The address is made by the elder who is supervising the sacrifice. In his hand he holds sacred leaves which he spits on as he talks. He is usually followed by the elders of other lineages who are attending the rite, and also by senior men who may not be elders but are important heads of families. Often they disagree about details of the lineage history or the particular sin that set off the sickness. But the main purpose of the address is to bring any lingering disputes and tensions into the open: because all must speak the truth as they see it this may lead to further arguments, but in the end equanimity is restored and all agree on the main points at issue.

After the second ritual address follow the rites of purification of the patient and his compound. Lugbara say that ghost invocation and consequent sacrifice to the ghosts are to "cleanse the territory" and to "cleanse the body," that is, to purify both lineage home and individual sinner. The sinner has been in both a state of sickness and a state of sin; the former is removed before the sacrifice is made, and the latter is removed by his blessing and anointment after the second ritual address is made. There are also many rites of purification that are performed without sacrifice.

The anointment and blessing of the sinner are done by the elders and important men of the lineage blowing into his ear, to "cool the sickness," and then by the spittle on the sacred leaves used in the ritual addresses being applied to his forehead, sternum, and insteps (the places where the soul is thought to enter and leave the body). The leaves are then placed on the shrines.

The last element in the sacrifice is the sharing of food among the living members of the congregation and the wider lineage. This is done in two parts. There is, first, the distribution of the meat among related lineages, and secondly, the sharing of cooked food by those who attend the rite itself. The raw meat that is distributed consists of the legs of the beast, with certain other parts of the body. They are divided under the supervision of the elder and given to the leaders of the closely related lineages attending the rite. These men take the meat home, and on the following day they in turn allocate it to their own closely related lineages, including accessory groups. The distribution of raw meat reflects the pattern of lineage ties centered upon the host lineage. Immediately after the distribution of raw meat has been made, the members of the congregation are given cooked meat, porridge, and beer, prepared by the wives of the host lineage. At this point the members of the congregation rearrange their position within the compound. Hitherto they have sat by lineage, but now they change to sit by generation. They are then served with food and beer. The sharing of food in this way by members of different minimal lineages but of the same generation or level of seniority—old men, "men behind," "big youths," youths—represents the unity of the wider lineage. Whereas the distinctness of each lineage and segment, related to common ancestry, is affirmed by its receiving a portion of raw meat, its unity with other segments is emphasized by the actual eating of cooked food jointly with them. Here the individual identities of segments are forgotten and their unity is stressed.

At the telling of the second ritual address, agreement is reached among the senior men present as to the exact genealogy of the group. At the sharing of sacrificial meat, men sit according to their kin relationships as stated in the genealogy. A genealogy is not necessarily historically true, although it may be so. It changes in time, some ancestors being forgotten and dropped out, and the ties between others being rearranged. It is in fact a means of expressing, and validating, patterns of authority among the living. The most powerful man is given the senior genealogical position. I have noticed, in even two years, changes being made in Lugbara genealogies; these are made at sacrifices. A genealogy is all that Lugbara have as a record of their lineage history and experience, so that part of the importance of sacrifice is that at it and by it history and experience are formulated and brought up to date, publicly stated and agreed upon, and both heard (in the address) and seen (in the seating arrangements) by all members of the lineage.

Witches and Sorcerers

Before considering the place of sacrifice in the total system of social relations and authority, it is useful to say something about Lugbara beliefs in witches and sorcerers. In Lugbara thought, these are closely connected with the cult of the dead, although there is no cult associated with them as such.

I use the classical distinction made by Evans-Pritchard between witches and sorcerers (Evans-Pritchard 1937, and Middleton and Winter 1963). Witchcraft is a mystical power by which some people are thought to be able to harm or kill others whom they dislike, whereas sorcery is the use of material objects (usually called "medicines") to harm or kill them. It may be accepted that witchcraft as such does not exist in actuality. It is the belief about it that is socially important. Sorcery may exist, as it is possible for people to use objects which they think may harm others (or poisons which may actually do so), but again it is the belief about it that is important. The beliefs about witches and sorcerers, even if scientifically unfounded, form a coherent system of thought that fits in with beliefs in the powers of the dead, Spirit, and other agents that can send sickness and disaster to human beings.

Witches and sorcerers are known generically as *oleu*, but the word is applied properly to witches only. The word comes from *ole*, meaning indignation or envy, and used in the term for ghost invocation, *ole ro*. A witch is thus a "man with indignation or envy." *Ole ro* means literally "to cause sickness because of indignation," and besides referring to invocation also means "to bewitch." The former activity is regarded as good and proper, the latter as evil. There are thought to be various forms of witches. They are always men. Some, the most common, "walk at night," often in the guise of a rat or other night animal, or as a moving light; others walk about and defecate blood on their victim's compound. In the morning the victim wakes up aching and sick, and may die unless the witch removes his witchcraft. Certain qualities are always ascribed to witches: they are said to be incestuous and cannibalistic, to be grey or even white in skin color, to have red eyes, and even to walk about upside-down. In short, they are given the inverted attributes which, as I have mentioned before, characterize the figures of myth. Clearly these qualities are axiomatic only, in the sense that a particular man thought to be a witch is unlikely to possess them. Such a man has attributes as, for example, being physically ugly or deformed, or being bad-tempered and grumpy. An ugly man may be merely a day-witch or evil-eye man; he is known by his physical appearance and therefore is not greatly feared. The witch who appears normal but whose personality and temperament are abnormal is the dangerous one. Such a man may live alone, eat alone, and be generally unfriendly and unneighborly; but he may also dissemble and be overhospitable and overfriendly to everyone. Lugbara say cynically that everyone hates someone in his heart, and so any man can be a witch. In short, a witch is a representation of the abnormal, unusual, or contrary, in terms of either physique or behavior.

No one knows how witchcraft actually works, but people understand a witch's motive, *ole*. It is said that a man feels envy at seeing others eat rich food when he has nothing, at seeing other men dancing and admired by women while he stands alone, or at seeing other men surrounded by kin and children when he has none of his own. But the sentiment of *ole* is more than mere envy. It is resentment at failing to achieve selfish personal ambition. In Lugbara, high status and prestige are traditionally acquired only, or almost only, through position in the lineage and by age, the two usually going together. It is true that a wealthy man can acquire followers, and if he is also wise or has a strong personality he may become a "man whose name is known." But typically he has to wait for genealogical position to become the head of a family and so a "man behind." Only a few can become elders, the heads of lineages, but all men wish to acquire this status. Lugbara realize that within the lineage there is ideally a fairly clearly defined and ordered system of authority; but they also know that not all men are willing to accept this system and wait for their proper turn to acquire lineage authority for themselves. They wish to circumvent the system, to acquire wealth and authority before their time, to refuse the proper authority of their seniors, to abuse their authority for their own ends instead of those of the lineage. An elder who is insulted and disobeyed by a junior is said to feel *ole* (indignation) because his status in the lineage is thereby dishonored; but an ambitious and selfish man who must obey a senior also feels *ole*, although in this case it is not indignation as such but rather envy or resentment at not getting his own way. Such a sentiment motivates witches. Lugbara are ambivalent about these matters. It is generally agreed that a senior man, and especially an elder, should be "slow," mindful of his responsibilities to his lineage and his dependents, careful not to regard a personal insult as an offense against his lineage authority. A witch is the opposite of an elder in this respect. People also realize that a witch is powerful, and that all men desire power; yet they they know that to acquire it by means of witchcraft for motives of personal ambition is "evil." Any man can be a witch, provided he is old enough. Witchcraft power is closely akin to legitimate lineage authority. In fact, it is seen as the same power but misapplied and abused. A man who is accused of witchcraft is offended and denies it; yet I have known many old men so accused who clearly were not averse to being credited with this power.

There are two main kinds of sorcerers who use material objects to harm others: *'ba enyanya beri* ("people with sorcery poison"), and *elojua*. The former are both men and women. The men are said to prepare poisons, from snakes and other evil creatures, which they sprinkle in their victims' food or drop in their compounds or fields; they can thus make their victims sick and even make them die, or harm crops and cattle. They do this because of envy of their victims' possessions. Women sorcerers are co-wives who are jealous of each other, and particularly of each others' children, whom they try to harm by using medicines prepared from the placentae of their co-wives' babies. *Elojua* are young men who are thought to buy poisons from the Congo and southern Uganda. When they return home they sprinkle them indiscriminately on the ground, particularly at markets, so that people become sick. Their motive is a general hatred of senior people who refuse to admire their new wealth from labor migration and who insist on their taking their proper junior lineage role. Sorcerers do not misuse lineage power, either because they are men jealous of neighbors (between whom there is no lineage tie and therefore no mystical tie of authority), or are women and young men, who have no lineage authority in any case.

Cult, Accusation, and Ambition

The process of sacrifice and the beliefs in the dead, Spirit, and witches, form a coherent system of thought. They do not occur in isolation. The behavior associated with them is part of the total behavior of people who see themselves as members of lineages, as neighbors, as important men, men who have ambitions they find difficult to realize, and so on. Lugbara believe in these various mystical powers and the agents who possess them, and use these beliefs in their relations with others, in attempts to better their positions in the lineage and neighborhood. Lugbara, like people anywhere, have ambitions for themselves, both as kinsmen out to help their own kin and as individuals out to help themselves—if necessary at the expense of their own kin. It is the conflict that so often arises between these two ambitions, the one laudable and good, the other selfish, that is at the basis of the operation of the cult I have described above. The relations between persons, which are expressed and controlled in terms of the cult of the dead and accusations of witchcraft, are relations of authority and power.

Although not all quarrels within the lineage and family cluster are between men (women are rarely directly concerned) who are concerned with the maintenance of lineage authority and the challenge made to it by men with overweening ambition, personal quarrels normally express underlying structural tensions. These are typically due to factors such as land shortage and population increase. Those disputes that are important in this sense are those that lead to the processes of ghost invocation and ghostly vengeance; purely personal quarrels tend to be resolved by fighting. I have noticed, from observation of many cases of sickness and sacrifice, that where the invoker is senior to the sick person the reason given for his invocation is usually disobedience to the authority of the senior man; but when the two parties are equal in generation and status the reason is usually impiety to the dead (followed often by ghostly vengeance). In the latter situation, however, it is common for the sickness to "strike" a dependent, such as a wife or child, who is regarded as a substitute for the offender.

Lugbara know that men are ambitious and want authority; a man who does not is regarded as weak and worthless. But men should be content with their proper authority, as defined by their lineage status, their age, and general social position. Many men, however, try to acquire authority that they should not have, to deny it to those who merit it, and to abuse it when they do acquire it. Old men die, and young men grow socially mature, and to say that men want authority is merely to state these facts in individual, psychological terms. For a man not to feel ambitious in this sense would show him to be immature. Lugbara say that once, "before the Europeans," men were content with their proper authority to a greater extent than they are today. This view should be seen in its historical context. The creation of paid and powerful chiefs and subchiefs gave to Lugbara an example, that was lacking in their traditional society, of men who rose to great power suddenly, and apparently without waiting to grow old and senior. Lugbara interpreted this phenomenon in terms that they could understand, that is, as the success of inordinately ambitious men who not only acquired undeserved power but also exercised it improperly merely by doing what the government expected of them (collecting taxes, demanding labor, and so on). There are also the younger men who go on labor migration to return with more money than they should have, by traditional Lugbara standards. Traditionally a man who appeared too ambitious would soon have been shown his place by force, or even have been killed, whereas today he can move away from angry kin and neighbors and be protected by the central government. Indeed, a wealthy trader or seller of cash crops is regarded by the government as progressive and worthy of support, while traditionally minded Lugbara see him as merely ambitious and undeserving.

By the cult of the dead conflicts over family and lineage authority may be played out without recourse to physical force. It is said of a senior man, "I cannot strike with my hand, the ghosts must strike for me." The axis of conflict over authority within the lineage and the family cluster changes in time, at various stages in the cycle of development of the cluster. In this cycle of development, the following five stages may usually be distinguished, at each of which a different pattern of authority, ghost invocation, and witchcraft accusations can be discerned.

1. The pattern of authority and genealogical relationships correspond closely, so that there is little argument over the exercise of authority between senior and junior or between the heads of component families.

2. Conflicts appear within domestic families, mainly as a consequence of the marriages of sons who therefore need land and livestock. For a time, however, these conflicts are soon settled by the heads of families who merely

allocate land and cattle; it is now that the lines of future conflicts become apparent.

3. In time the population of the group increases and the fertility of its land may decline. Older men die and younger men mature, marry, and have children who ultimately marry and need land in their turn. Conflicts of authority arise, both between the lineage elder and the heads of families, and also between these heads of families and their sons. As the authority of the senior men is questioned more and more, they have to use the authority of the dead (by invocation) to enforce their own authority. Some junior men may move away at this stage, to attach themselves to other family clusters.

4. The conflicts increase in both seriousness and frequency, and are expressed ritually in two main ways. One is that the elder and other senior men no longer merely invoke the ghosts against their own dependants to maintain their own authority, but compete against one another. They do this by attempting to invoke the dead against each other's dependants. The elder is the principal intermediary between the living and the dead, but to a lesser extent this is so also for any man whose father is dead and thus a ghost. Hence, if a man can show that the dead have listened to his invocation against a dependant of one of his rivals in the lineage, this is tantamount to their showing that they have confidence in him alone, and no confidence in his rival. The actions of the dead are known to men, of course, only through oracles, so that rival senior men try themselves to consult the oracles and obtain oracular verdicts favorable to themselves. This may sound as though they deliberately cheat, but I do not think this is so. The matter is more subtle than that, for the simple reason that these men themselves believe in the truth of oracles. It is here that we may see the importance of the oracle operators, who are expected to sum up the general situation of conflict within the family cluster and return oracular verdicts that will express correctly the general opinion of the members of the family cluster. Only a sensitive and honest operator can do this, and in my experience the best-known operators are such men; the man who consults one of these operators and receives a verdict favorable to him gains his point.

The other way in which conflicts are expressed is by accusations of witchcraft. These follow two patterns. The first occurs when young men become sick because of ghost invocation by their elders: the young men say that the old men are jealous of them and bewitch them. No one takes this very seriously. Later, however, men of equal status, the heads of families, may accuse one another of being witches. This happens when one such man claims to invoke the ghosts against the dependants of a rival: the rival refuses to accept this version and says instead that the invoker has practiced witchcraft. As I have mentioned earlier, the Lugbara term for both processes is the same (*ole ro*), yet one is regarded as laudable, the other as evil. It is rare for a man actually to say his rival is a witch, as such; rather he says that the rival is "strong," or "walks at night," or some such phrase that implies witchcraft, and if he finds that the members of the family cluster agree with him, he grows bolder until he may finally have opinion on his side that the rival is indeed a witch. As a witch, he would be unsuitable to be a responsible senior member of the group and should be driven out and his authority disobeyed; and even if he has oracular verdicts on his side it can always be said that he has merely bewitched the oracles to give false verdicts. The position of an elder of whom this is said is difficult, because he finds his authority being increasingly disregarded and challenged. His only response is to increase his claims to have invoked the dead against unruly dependants, and if he does this too much he risks even more to be condemned as a witch. There are many variations on this pattern; but in general it may be said that fear of being thought a witch stops a senior man from being too overbearing and abusing his powers of invocation, and that a group within which there is much conflict being played out in ritual terms may appear to outsiders and members alike to be riddled by witchcraft. Witchcraft is a symptom and expression of dissension and tension.

5. Finally, the group segments into two or more new lineages. This occurs typically only at the death of an elder who has managed to hold the group together while alive. If the elder has held the status for only a few years, or if the group has not increased in number or still has plenty of land, it is unlikely to segment. The succession of a new elder is not marked by any particular rite or ceremony. But sooner or later he makes a sacrifice at shrines set for the earliest ghosts of the lineage and which are placed in the bushland away from the homesteads. Only lineage elders may go to these shrines or attend rites at them. They are regarded as "big" and dangerous, and a man is shown to be a true elder because the ghosts accept his right to sacrifice to them at one of these shrines. Once he does so, he thereby shows that he has truly succeeded to the office.

The Prophetic Cult of Yakan

I have given only an outline of the traditional religious system of the Lugbara. During my stay among them they still practiced the rites I have mentioned, although many young men and women had little time for them. But those older men who were Christians still either practiced these rites without making it too obvious to the missionaries or permitted their kin to practice them without hindrance. They realized that these rites were an integral part of Lugbara culture, and were not willing to see them forgotten. But the younger people who have gone to mission schools either believe that the old religion should be abandoned, or have merely lost interest in a cult that is closely linked to a traditional system of lineage and family authority which has itself been changing radically and which they find irksome. It is probably the general pattern of economic and social change that has weakened the traditional cults, rather than mission evangelism as such—although this is not to deny the sincerity of mission endeavor or the benefits that missions have brought to the Lugbara.

We cannot now reconstruct the details of Lugbara religion as it was a century ago, despite my use of the word "traditional." In this century there have appeared various other cults, as responses to external change, which have been in conflict with the cult of the dead. The most famous was the cult known as Yakan. I have described this cult at length elsewhere (Middleton 1963) but a few words about it are relevant here.

The cult was spread by prophets, who were Kakwa living to the north of Lugbaraland. About 1892 they were visited by some important Lugbara men who wished to be protected against meningitis, rinderpest, and the attacks of Arab slavers and Europeans. They obtained "the water of Yakan" and returned with it to distribute it to their followers. These men were later made chiefs by the Belgian administrator, as I have mentioned earlier. They were reappointed chiefs by the British in 1913. After 1913 the government became more efficient and affected everyday life to a far greater extent than previously. In addition, there were again serious epidemics of meningitis, rinderpest, and, later, Spanish influenza. The Lugbara reacted by turning once more to the Kakwa prophets. This time, however, the principal prophet, Rembe, entered Lugbaraland and traveled around the country dispensing his Yakan water. He was deported and executed in the Sudan about 1917. In 1919 the northeastern Lugbara revolted under local Yakan leaders. After defeat by police the cult ceased, and most of the government chiefs were implicated and deported. Since then the cult in its original form has died out, and today it exists as one of several spirit cults.

There are two main points about the Yakan cult that may be mentioned here. One is that the prophet Rembe was thought to come in some way from the Creator Spirit and the water to get its power from Spirit. Rembe was a charismatic leader whose power was thought to be divine and above control or even query by ordinary men. The other point is that Rembe introduced a new principle of organization into Lugbara society. Wherever he went the people to whom he personally gave water were known as "chiefs" (opi) of Yakan. They had a second grade of dispensers and officials, and the mass of adherents formed the third and lowest grade. Both men and women joined the cult, and in some areas membership was compulsory. People who drank the water were promised everlasting life, the return to earth of ancestors and cattle killed by rinderpest, and rifles with which to drive the Europeans away. Rembe himself told them not to harm Europeans, who would merely go away and leave the country in a state of primeval happiness and peace. The adherents lived in camps in the bushland, where men slept with women irrespective of clan affiliation. This form of organization, in which neither clan nor to a lesser extent age or sex were basic principles, was very different to and in important respects the very opposite of the traditional form. The promise to bring the ancestors back to earth would have destroyed the basis both of a cult of the dead and the authority of the living elders who were seen as intermediaries between the living and the dead. At first the rainmakers kept aloof from the movement, but toward the end they became "chiefs" of the cult, thus keeping their high ritual position.

The cult died out after 1919. This was, of course, to some extent due to the physical defeat of its adherents and the deportation of the leaders. But there were deeper reasons that prevented a reappearance of the cult. The mass of its adherents were ordinary men and women who found in it the opportunity to free themselves from the authority of their seniors. It seems that during the dozen or so years of disturbance caused by the imposition of colonial rule and the appearance of epidemics, the senior men had to impose their authority over their dependents more and more strictly. This was resented by the younger men, who also had the example of the suddenly rich and powerful chiefs as people who had been able to acquire much power and wealth without having the usual genealogical status. One way in which younger men could rid themselves of what they considered the irksome authority of their seniors was to join the cult. But when its organization was destroyed, alternatives were already appearing. Rather than try to resurrect the cult, young men found the new chances of moving from one part of the country to another or of going to southern Uganda as labor migrants. In either case they could become free of lineage authority, at least temporarily; and if they went south as laborers they could earn money and become to some extent economically independent of their elders.

Today the cult of Yakan still exists, but in a changed form. Yakan is conceived as a power that comes from Spirit and "seizes" men and makes them tremble and talk incoherently. Older men have shrines to Yakan in their compounds and make offerings to it when the sickness appears among their own dependants. Yakan is regarded as one of several spirits that can send this kind of sickness to people; it lacks the moral content of sickness sent by the dead. Some of these spirits are associated with lightning, earthquakes, and other natural phenomena, and others are connected with Christianity. Of these latter the best known is a spirit referred to as *balokole,* which comes from the Ganda word *Abalokole,* the name of a breakaway Christian sect which sent evangelists to Lugbara from Buganda in the 1940s. Lugbara say that because these evangelists go into a trance when possessed by God they must be suffering from a sickness sent by the Creator Spirit. Both Yakan and *balokole* are representations of the external powers which have affected Lugbara society in recent years of rapid social change: by making them into spirits whose power comes from the Creator Spirit, Lugbara believe that they can to some extent control them and therefore also control the external forces which in their view wish to destroy traditional Lugbara society and its culture.

□ **8** □

Conclusion: The Changing Society

I HAVE DESCRIBED the Lugbara as they were during my stay, except for the accounts of feud and warfare, which belong to the past. Their traditional form of social organization is a highly fragmentary one, very small in scale and lacking any obvious political authority above the level of small local groups. They have today, as in the past, a high density of population, yet they have been able effectively to control the continual squabbling and competition between local groups for land, grazing, and water. The great use made of religious sanctions has clearly kept large-scale violence at a minimum, as is no doubt necessary for people living so close together: too much fighting would have led to a state of near-anarchy. In addition, except for tracts for new fields there was little worth fighting for, since livestock have never played a very important part in Lugbara economy. In this respect the Lugbara contrast strikingly with the Nuer.

The organization of Lugbara society has undergone various changes, as a consequence of economic factors and the appearance of Europeans and a colonial administration. The first major change of which we have any knowledge occurred at the beginning of the colonial period. The Lugbara responded by having recourse to prophets, and attempted to form a new kind of organization that would do away with the traditional lineage system and replace it with one based on the "grades" of the Yakan cult. As I have said, this was not successful and the cult and its organization died out.

Since then there have been four main developments. One was the appointment of chiefs, described in Chapter 4. Another has been the emigration of young men to the richer parts of southern Uganda, mainly to Bunyoro and Buganda. Men go to work as unskilled laborers and sharecroppers. Most of them return after a year or so with a few pounds in earnings and such items as blankets and bicycles. Most men return south later for another spell but ultimately return to their lineage homes and settle down. A few migrants remain in the south and become "lost" to their kin. Very few Lugbara women go south,

89

because their men prefer to leave them at home away from the temptations of the modern world.

The migrants go to work on sugar and sisal plantations owned by Indians, as laborers in Kampala, the capital, and on Ganda farms; they also take up plots on a sharecropping basis in Buganda and Bunyoro. They live in settlements from which they go out to work daily, both on their own plots and as laborers for local landowners. They have a reputation as tough, hard-working, and unruly people and have little close contact with the people among whom they live. They grow cotton, the main cash crop of Uganda. These settlements are usually long-standing, and consist of Lugbara men under the control of a permanent resident who acts as their representative vis-à-vis the local population, and of women from local tribes. Each settlement is associated with a particular subtribe in Lugbaraland, and contact is maintained both between the settlements and between them and the homeland.

It is often said that the effect of labor migration is purely destructive of the traditional way of life, and this is no doubt true of the Lugbara to some extent. On the other hand, it has enabled them to maintain a density of population which is often higher than the land could otherwise bear; and it brings in money which in this area, remote from industrial and commercial centers, would otherwise be difficult to obtain. The temporary absence of young men has eased the pressure on the land (as I have said, the higher the density of population the higher the proportion of absentees). Young men may go south to escape the discipline of parents and chiefs, but most of them are told to go by their elders. An elder decides how much money his family will need in the immediate future, mainly for taxation and the purchase of bridewealth animals, and sends enough men to earn it. They are supposed to return most of their earnings to the elder, but of course many try to keep their money, mainly by remitting it to their mothers' brothers, who will keep it for them. Old men complain that their juniors are selfish and do not help their families; young men grumble at what they see as the rapacity of their elders, who may use the money on their own pleasures and on their favorites. There is much justification on both sides, and the main consequence is an increasing disregard of the elders' authority and its religious sanctions. The cult of the dead is weakened by economic factors as much as by mission teaching.

With this has gone an atomization of the formerly large family clusters. Men earn money and resent its going to members of other elementary families, even if they are of the same family cluster. Also the physical dispersal of large compounds which was mentioned in Chapter 1 has tended to alter the traditional system. An elementary family is economically less viable than the large family cluster, since in the large group the wives can make one another loans and gifts of grain to tide them over temporary shortage. They are less willing to do this when living in separate homesteads with often widely separated fields. The growth of markets is important here. Markets have appeared in Lugbaraland only since about 1925, and most of the traders in them are women exchanging small local surpluses and maize used for beer brewing. Traditionally they would merely have distributed surpluses to co-wives and kin as kinship gifts. Markets are also a means of distributing cash and consumer goods, and the many small traders who have opened shops in Lugbaraland have played similar roles (Middleton 1962).

The third development has been cash-crop growing. Since the introduction of taxation in the early days of colonial rule, Lugbara have had to find money for it, and they also need money for the purchase of modern consumer goods. Their country is too high for growing cotton, and various substitutes have been tried, such as simsim, groundnuts, and sunflower oil, but none has been successful due to the distance of their country from export markets. However, hides and skins and tobacco have been worth exporting, and the sale of these, and labor migration, have been the main sources of cash (there is virtually no local employment for wages). Until the late 1940s, cash was obtained mostly through labor migration, but in the 1950s tobacco-growing became increasingly important. There have been small foreign-owned tobacco factories in Lugbaraland for many years. They issue seed and buy the leaf for curing and export. In the 1950s tobacco cooperatives were set up for the drying of local leaf. Tobacco used to be grown in small amounts by every family cluster, the elder taking the money after sale of the leaf and using it for the benefit of the cluster as a whole. The cooperatives have had an effect on this pattern, however, inasmuch as they are mostly sited away from the closely settled areas and their members have been the younger men. Consequently young men are able to acquire their own money and usually refuse to give it to their elders. Along with the increase in this kind of tobacco-growing has gone a decrease in labor migration, although as yet this is not very marked. But it seems clear that in the future Lugbara will earn more of their money at home instead of outside their own country.

Labor migration and cash-crop growing, together with the appearance of chiefs and traders, have led to the last development, that of an incipient new class of people who gain their livelihood by earning wages or selling produce instead of by traditional subsistence farming. These are the "New People" ('ba odiru). The more important New People are the educated and semieducated protégés of the government and the missions, and the wealthier traders. They are men who come into contact with Europeans and other foreigners. They attend the same schools; they live in brick houses and adopt a Western way of life; their families intermarry and many of them have ties with similar people outside Lugbaraland. These men are Lugbara and therefore have intimate ties with Lugbara society, but as New People their loyalties are to members of their class, as well as to members of their own lineages and families. The leaders of this class provide a new example for the aspiring younger men who can earn money from labor migration or cash-cropping. The traditional ideal of slowly becoming a respected elder by merely growing old and acquiring lineage seniority, a necessarily slow process, is giving way to that of acquiring power and position outside the lineage system. To achieve this a man needs wealth, education, perhaps a job with the government or missions, and a willingness to deny many of the traditional ties with lineage and family. Many—perhaps most—of these men have seen southern Uganda as labor migrants, and the elder among them were soldiers in the second world war and saw countries outside East Africa. They consider themselves to be the vanguard of social and political progress. The older people who see modern developments in a different light—as stages in the progressive and regrettable destruction of Lugbara culture—call them *Mundu* and bewail their growing importance. But the older people are dying out, and the New People are clearly the men of the future.

References

CRAZZOLARA, J. P., 1950–54, *The Lwoo*. 3 volumes, Verona: Museum Cambonianum.

EVANS-PRITCHARD, E. E., 1937, *Witchcraft, oracles and magic among the Azande*. New York: Oxford University Press.

——, 1940, *The Nuer*. New York: Oxford University Press.

——, 1951, *Kinship and marriage among the Nuer*. New York: Oxford University Press.

FORTES, M., and E. E. EVANS-PRITCHARD, 1940, *African political systems*. London: Oxford University Press.

MIDDLETON, J., 1955, "Notes on the political organization of the Madi of Uganda," *African Studies*, 14 (1).

——, 1960a, "The Lugbara," in A. I. Richards (ed.), *East African chiefs*, London: Faber & Faber, Ltd.

——, 1960b, *Lugbara religion: ritual and authority among an East African people*. London: Oxford University Press.

——, 1962, "Trade and markets in Lugbara," in P. Bohannan and G. Dalton (eds.), *Markets in Africa*. Evanston, Ill.: Northwestern University Press.

——, 1963, "The Yakan or Allah Water cult among the Lugbara," *Journal of the Royal Anthropological Institute*, 93 (1).

MIDDLETON, J., and TAIT D. (eds.), 1958, *Tribes without rulers*. London: Routledge & Kegan Paul Ltd.

MIDDLETON, J., and WINTER E. H. (eds.), 1963, *Witchcraft and sorcery in East Africa*. London: Routledge & Kegan Paul Ltd.

RAMPONI, E., 1937, "Religion and divination of the Logbara tribe of North-Uganda" *Anthropos*, 32.

RICHARD, A. I. (ed.), 1956, *Migrant labour and tribal life*. Cambridge: W. Heffer & Sons, Ltd.

SOUTHALL, A. W., 1956, *Alur society*. Cambridge: W. Heffer & Sons, Ltd.

STIGAND, C. H., 1923, *Equatoria, the Lado Enclave*. London: Constable & Co., Ltd.

TUCKER, A. N., 1940, *The Eastern Sudanic languages*. London: Oxford University Press.

Further Reading

BAXTER, B. T. W., and A. BUTT, *The Azande and related peoples*. London: International African Institute, 1953.

This volume in the *Ethnographic Survey of Africa* gives a summary of the available information about the peoples of the culture area to which the Lugbara belong. It deals mostly with the Azande.

CRAZZOLARA, J. P., *The Lwoo*. 3 volumes. Verona: Museum Cambonianum, 1950–1954.

Father Crazzolara's knowledge of the myths, traditions, and history of the peoples of this region is unrivaled. Although the Lugbara and Madi are not Lwoo peoples they were the autochthonous inhabitants of the area.

EVANS-PRITCHARD, E. E., *Witchcraft, oracles and magic among the Azande*. New York: Oxford University Press, 1937.

The classic study of African witchcraft and the only detailed account of any other people of this culture area.

MIDDLETON, J., "Notes on the political organization of the Madi of Uganda," *African Studies,* 14 (1), 1955.

The only account of Madi social organization.

MIDDLETON, J., *Lugbara religion: ritual and authority among an East African people*. London: Oxford University Press, 1960.

A full-length study of Lugbara religion and its place in their culture.

MIDDLETON, J., and D. TAIT (eds.), *Tribes without rulers*. London: Routledge & Kegan Paul Ltd., 1958.

Contains short accounts of the political systems of several African peoples of a type similar to the Lugbara. It includes papers on the Lugbara, Dinka, and Mandari, all in the same region.

NALDER, L. F., *A tribal survey of Mongalla province*. London: Oxford University Press, 1937.

A valuable survey of the peoples of the southwestern Sudan, many of which are closely related to the Lugbara.

RICHARDS, A. I., *East African chiefs.* London: Faber & Faber, Ltd., 1960.
    Contains accounts of the development of modern chiefship among many
    East African peoples, including the Lugbara and Alur.
SELIGMAN, C. G. and B. Z., *Pagan tribes of the Nilotic Sudan.* London: Rout-
    ledge Ltd., 1932.
    The most important survey of the peoples of the southern Sudan.
SOUTHALL, A. W., *Alur society.* Cambridge: W. Seffer & Sons, Ltd., 1956.
    A full account of the Alur, the southerly neighbors of the Lugbara.

Glossary

AFFINAL, AFFINE: People related through marriage, "in-laws."

AGNATE: A patrilineal kinsman, i.e., one related through men only.

CASSAVA: Manioc (*Manihot utilissima*). A short-term perennial root crop. It has a high yield but poor food value.

CLAN: A group of kin with a common founding ancestor or ancestress; descent from the founder is either through men only (patrilineal or agnatic) or women only (matrilineal).

ELEUSINE: Finger millet (*Eleusine coracana*). A small grain plant that can be stored for a long period and is a valuable source of vegetable protein.

ENSORCELL: To practice sorcery.

EXOGAMY: The rule by which members of a group (usually a clan or lineage) must marry outside the group.

LINEAGE: A group of kin descended from a common ancestor through men only (patrilineal or agnatic) or women only (matrilineal). It differs from a clan in that the members can trace their exact genealogical relationship, whereas those of a clan cannot do so but merely recognize their common ancestry. A *minimal lineage* is the smallest lineage recognized.

POLYGYNY: A form of marriage in which a man can have more than one wife at the same time.

SIMSIM: Sesame (*Sesamum indicum*). A small grain that yields a valuable cooking-oil.

SORGHUM: "Great millet" (*Sorghum vulgare*). A large grain plant.

TRANSHUMANCE: The seasonal moving of herds from one grazing ground to another, in a regular cycle.

UTERINE KIN: Kin related through women, such as mothers' brothers and sisters' children.